How to Become Money

Workbook

ACCESS CONSCIOUSNESS®

"All of Life Comes to Us with Ease, Joy and Glory!®"

Gary M. Douglas

Published by Access Consciousness Publishing, LLC

www.accessconsciousnesspublishing.com

Printed in the United States of America

ACCESS CONSCIOUSNESS

"All of life comes to me with EASE & JOY & GLORY

Table of Contents

CHAPTER ONE: What is money? 21

CHAPTER TWO: What does money mean to you?... 37

CHAPTER THREE: What three emotions do you have when you think of money? 51

CHAPTER FOUR: What does money feel like to you?....................................... 74

CHAPTER FIVE: What does money look like to you?..85

CHAPTER SIX: What does money taste like to you? 86

CHAPTER SEVEN: When you see money coming toward you, from which direction do you feel it coming? 91

CHAPTER EIGHT: In relationship to money, do you feel you have more than you need or less than you need? 94

CHAPTER NINE: In relationship to money, when you close your eyes, what color is it and how many dimensions does it have? 96

CHAPTER TEN: In relationship to money, what is easier, inflow or outflow? 98

CHAPTER ELEVEN: What are your three worst problems with money?............................100

CHAPTER TWELVE: Which do you have more of, money or debts? 105

CHAPTER THIRTEEN: In relationship to money, to have an abundance of money in your life, what three things would be a solution to your current financial situation?.................................. 107

Introduction

Gary Douglas (founder of Access Consciousness®) originally channeled this information from a being called Raz. Gary no longer channels. This is a transcription of a live class.

Access is about empowering you to know what you know. It's about awareness. You are the one that knows what is right for you.

Please use this book as a tool to facilitate the insane and limited points of view you have created around money, and to create more ease in your life and living with a lot more money and currency flows.

For more information on Access Consciousness®, and for more products and classes on all subjects of life - business, money, relationships, sex, magic, bodies and more - please go to our website. Do and be whatever it takes to create and generate YOUR life and living to be more than you ever perceived possible!

www.accessconsciousness.com

Transcript From A Live Class With Gary Douglas Channelling A Being Called Raz

Gary: This workshop on money will be a new experience for me. I don't know how it will be for you. Make sure you all have your notebooks, your pens or pencils, whatever you're going to use because you're going to have a lot to do here tonight. From the little that the Raz gave me, there's going to be a lot that's going to be happening. Once again he's going to ask you to volunteer to step up to the front and to be the mirror for other people here. So, if you have a problem with that, put a blanket around yourself so he can't see you, otherwise he's going to ask you. And don't be embarrassed by anything that goes on because the reality is there isn't a person in here who doesn't have exactly the same problem you do in one form or another. It doesn't make any difference whether you've got a million dollars or fifty cents, the issues of money are tough ones for everybody. Okay? So here we go.

Workbook Questions

Tonight we are going to talk about how to **BE** money. That which you are is energy. That which you will be is energy. That which you have been is energy. That which is money is energy.

As you, this night, answer the questions that we are going to ask, be in awareness that the honesty of your answers relates not to the people around you, but to self. Every point of view that you have created about money creates the limitations and parameters from which you receive it.

Everything that you create, others create. Be in total honesty with self, otherwise you are the only one you are fooling; everybody else will know your secrets anyway.

We ask you to remember that the subject we are now dealing with is not one that is considered light, but it should be. Light is funny, it is a joke, you can laugh, it is all right. So be prepared to be the en-lightened beings that you are.

If you truly desire results in this, it would be best if you answered all these questions in this section before moving onto the next chapter.

Rasputin: 'Allo

Students: Good evening, Rasputin.

R: How are you? So, this evening we are going to speak about that which is most dear to all your hearts, that which is money. And it is, that for each of you, money is not the issue that you think it is, but we are going to work with you to assist you in beginning to learn how to cope with money, not as a moment-by-moment situation, but as the allowance of the abundance that is the truth of self that you are.

So, we will begin. We ask you the question: What is money? And you write three answers of what money is to you. Now, do not put down what you think it should be, do not put down the 'right' answer because there is no such thing. Allow your brains to float away and allow that which is the truth of where you sit to be the answer on the page. So, three things that money is to you.

QUESTION ONE: What is money?

Answer 1:

_____

_____

_____

_____

Answer 2:

_____

_____

_____

_____

Answer 3:

_____

_____

_____

_____

Okay, everybody ready? The second question is: What does money mean to you? Write down three answers.

QUESTION TWO: What does money mean to you?

Answer 1:

_____

_____

_____

_____

Answer 2:

_____

_____

_____

_____

Answer 3:

_____

_____

_____

_____

Third question: What three emotions do you have when you think of money?

QUESTION THREE: What three emotions do you have when you think of money?

Answer 1:

_____

_____

_____

_____

Answer 2:

_____

_____

_____

_____

Answer 3:

_____

_____

_____

_____

Now, next question, question number four: What does money feel like to you? Three answers. What does money feel like to you?

QUESTION FOUR: What does money feel like to you?

Answer 1:

_____

_____

_____

_____

Answer 2:

_____

_____

_____

_____

Answer 3:

_____

_____

_____

_____

Next question: What does money look like to you?

QUESTION FIVE: What does money look like to you?

Answer 1:

_____

_____

_____

_____

Answer 2:

_____

_____

_____

_____

Answer 3:

_____

_____

_____

_____

Everybody ready? Next question: What does money taste like to you? Feel it in your mouth. What does it taste like? Now most of you have not had money in your mouth since you were small children, so you can use that as a point of reference.

QUESTION SIX: What does money taste like to you?

Answer 1:

_____

_____

_____

_____

Answer 2:

_____

_____

_____

_____

Answer 3:

_____

_____

_____

_____

Next question, everybody ready? Next question is: When you see money coming toward you, from which direction do you feel it coming? From the right, from the left, from the back, from the front, from up, from down, from all around? Where do you see it coming from?

QUESTION SEVEN: When you see money coming toward you, from which direction do you feel it coming?

Answer 1:

_____

_____

_____

_____

Answer 2:

_____

_____

_____

_____

Answer 3:

_____

_____

_____

_____

All right, next question: In relationship to money, do you feel you have more than you need or less than you need?

QUESTION EIGHT: In relationship to money, do you feel you have more than you need or less than you need?

Answer:

_____

_____

_____

_____

Next: In relationship to money, when you close your eyes, what color is it and how many dimensions does it have?

QUESTION NINE: In relationship to money, when you close your eyes, what color is it and how many dimensions does it have?

Answer 1:

_____

_____

_____

_____

Answer 2:

_____

_____

_____

_____

Answer 3:

_____

_____

_____

_____

QUESTION TEN: In relationship to money, what is easier, inflow or outflow?

Answer:

_____

_____

_____

_____

Next question: What are your three worst problems with money?

QUESTION ELEVEN: What are your three worst problems with money?

Answer 1:

_____

_____

_____

_____

Answer 2:

_____

_____

_____

_____

Answer 3:

_____

_____

_____

_____

Next question: Which do you have more of, money or debts?

QUESTION TWELVE: Which do you have more of money or debts?

Answer:

_____

_____

_____

_____

We are going to give you one other question: In relationship to money, to have abundance of money in your life, what three things would be a solution to your current financial situation?

QUESTION THIRTEEN: In relationship to money, to have an abundance of money in your life, what three things would be a solution to your current financial situation?

Answer 1:

_____

_____

_____

_____

Answer 2:

_____

_____

_____

_____

Answer 3:

_____

_____

_____

_____

All right, everybody got their answers? Anybody not got answers? All right, now, go back to the beginning of your page, read the questions through and ask yourself if you have been totally honest about your answers and that these are the ones you wish to have on the page. If not, change them.

Look at your answers and decide if you have created them in honesty, honesty with self. There are no right answers, there are no wrong answers, there are only points of view; that is all there are, points of view. And they are the limitations from which you have created your life. If you are functioning from what is the cosmic right answer, you are not being truthful with self, because if you were, your life would be quite different.

What is money? For some money is cars, for some money is houses, for some money is security, for some money is an exchange of energy. But, is it those things? No, it is not. It is energy, as are you energy. There is no difference between you and money except the points of view that you give it. And you give it those points of view because you have bought the points of view of others.

If you would change that which is your financial situation, if you would change that which is money in your life, then you must learn to be allowance in all things. But in particular, when you hear a point of view delivered to you, you must look to it and see if it is true for you. If it is true for you, you have made an alignment or agreement and you have made it solidity. If it is not true for you, you either resist or react to it and you have made it solidity. Even your own points of view need no agreement, they need be only interesting points of view.

What you are, what you would have, you must BE. That which you do not have in you, you cannot have at all. If you see money as outside of you, you cannot have it. If you see money anywhere besides within the being of you, you will never have it at all and there will never be enough from your point of view.

$$$$$$$$$$$$$$$$$$$$$$

CHAPTER ONE

What is money?

Rasputin: All right, so everybody ready? All done? All satisfied with your answers? All right. So now we begin to speak about money. To begin, you now have an understanding, from what you have put down upon your page, of your own points of view about money. You see your life as the financial situation that you are in, you buy the point of view that your life is what you have now, as financial reality. Interesting point of view.

Now, we speak, as we have many times, once again, about the difference between allowance and acceptance. Allowance: You are the rock in the stream and any thought, idea, belief or decision comes at you, goes around you and moves on, if you are the rock in the stream and you are in allowance. If you are in acceptance, all ideas, thoughts, beliefs, decisions come at you and you become part of the stream and you get washed away.

Acceptance has three components: alignment or agreement, which makes it a solidity, resistance, which makes it a solidity, and reaction, which makes it a solidity. How does that look in real life? Well, if your friend says to you, "There is just not enough money in the world." If you align or agree with it you go, "Yes, you are right," and you make that a solidity in his life and your own. If you resist it, you think, "This guy wants money from me," and you make it a solidity, in his life and your own. If you react to it, you say, "Well, I have plenty of money in my life, I don't know what is wrong with you," or you say, "That is not the way it is going to be for me", and you have bought it, you have paid for it and taken it home in a bag and you have made it solidity for yourself.

If your friend says to you, "There is not enough money in the world" that is only an interesting point of view. Every time you hear information about money, you must instantly acknowledge that it is only an interesting point of view; it does not have to be your reality, it does not have to be what occurs. If you think it is easier to borrow than to pay back, then you have made it a solidity and you have created continuous debt. It is only an interesting point of view, after all.

What is money? Well, some of you think money is gold, some of you think money is cars, some of you think money is houses, some of you think money is energy exchange, some of you think it is a medium of exchange. Notice each of those points of view is a solidity. Money is only energy. There is nothing in the world, nothing, that is not energy.

If you look at your lives and you think you have not enough money, you are really saying to the angels that sit with you, that assist you, you are telling them that you do not need additional money, you do not need energy. In truth, you do not need, you are energy and you have no limited supply of it at all. You have more than enough energy to do everything you desire in your life, but you do not choose to create yourselves as money, as energy, as power.

What is power to you? For most of you power is about overwhelming another, or it is about controlling another, or it is about controlling your life, or putting controls in your life, or controlling your financial destiny. Interesting point of view, eh?

Financial destiny, what is that? It is a weird program, that is what it is, a program of fate. Every time you say, "I have to have a program of financial freedom," you are telling yourself that you, personally, have no freedom. And, therefore, you have limited, in totality, your choices and what you experience.

We ask you all, at the moment to close your eyes and to begin to pull energy from the front of you, pull it in to every pore of your body. Not breathe it in, just pull it in. Good, and now pull it in from the back of you, from everywhere. And now pull it in from the sides of you and now pull it in from the bottom of you. Notice there is plenty of energy available to you when you pull it in. Now, turn it into money. Notice how most of you made it very dense all of a sudden. No longer was it energy that you were pulling in, it was something significant. You have bought the idea that money is a significance, and therefore, you have made it a solidity, you have aligned with the agreement of the rest of the world that is how it functions, it functions on energy. The world does not function on money, the world functions on energy. The world pays in coin of energy and if you are giving and receiving of money as energy, you will have abundance.

But for most of you, inflowing of energy is the category, it is the idea. Pull energy again into the totality of your body, pull it in, pull it in. Can you hold onto it? Does it seem to build and get more and more? Does it stop with you? No, you just are energy and the direction in which you focus your attention is how you create energy. Money is the same.

Now, everything in the world is energy. There is no place that you can't receive energy from. You can receive energy from the dog shit on the ground, from the pee in snow or you can feel it from the car or the taxi driver. There, are you all picking it up? You receive energy from everywhere. Now, take the taxi driver and flow massive amounts of money out the front of you towards the taxi driver, any taxi driver will do. Flow it out, more, more, more, more, more, more, more. Now, feel the energy that is pulling in the back side of you. Are you limiting the amount of energy that is coming in the back side?

Where does money come from? If you see it coming from the right or the left you are seeing that your life is about working, because this is the only way that you can get money. If you are seeing it coming from the front of you, you are seeing it as belonging to the future. And if you are seeing it from behind you, you are seeing that it comes from that which is the past. And this is the only place you have had money. Your life is about, "I had money, now I have none, so I am very pathetic." Not reality, only an interesting point of view.

Now, when you flow money, do you flow it from your heart chakra, your root chakra, or your crown chakra, where do you flow it from? You flow it from everywhere, the totality of your being and then it flows in from the totality of your being.

If you see money coming from the top of you, then you think that spirit is to provide you with money. Spirit provides you with energy, energy to create anything you decide to create. What do you do, what do you do, to create money? First of all, you must become power. Power is not sitting on top of another, power is not controlling. Power is energy... unlimited, expansive, growing, magnificent, glorious, fabulous, exuberant and quick energy. It is everywhere, there is no diminishment of self in energy, there is no diminishment of self in power and there is no diminishment of another. When you are being power, you are in totality – self! And when you are self, you are being energy, and as energy, all is connected to you, which means unlimited supplies of money are connected as well.

Now, you will become power and to do that you say, ten times in the morning "I am power." And in the evening you say ten times, "I am power." What else must you be? Creativity. "I am creativity." What is creativity? Creativity is the vision of your life and the work that you desire to do as the essence of you, as the soul of energy. Everything that you do, done at creativity, regardless of whether you are sweeping the floor, cleaning the toilets, washing the windows, washing the dishes, cooking the meal, writing the checks, done as creativity connected to power, equals energy, and results in money, because they are all the same then.

The next element you must have is that which is awareness. What is awareness? Awareness is the recognition that everything, everything that you think, gets created. It is manifested. It is how your life shows up by your thoughts alone.

If you have the creative image of where you are going and what you are going to do and you attach to it the awareness that is a done deal, it will manifest. But what you do upon this plane is, you add in the element of time – time! Time is your killer because if you do not manifest a million dollars tomorrow, after completing this course tonight, you will decide it is a worthless class and you will forget everything you learned.

Well, how do you account for time? By being control. "I am control."

What does it mean to be "I am control"? "I am control" is the understanding that at the correct time, in the correct way, without your defining the path, that which you envision as creativity, that which you are aware of as a completion, that which you connected to as the power of it, as the energy of it, is a done deal in its own time, in its own framework. And, if you put those four components together and you allow the universe to adjust every aspect of it, to fine-tune the world to become your slave, you will manifest exactly what you desire.

Now, let us talk about desire for a minute. Desire is the emotion from which you decide to create. Is it a reality? No, it is only an interesting point of view. If you desire clothes, do you do it for a reason or because you are cold or because you are too hot or because you have worn out your shoes? No, you do not do it for that reason, you do it for many others. Because someone has told you that you look good in that color or because somebody said they have seen you once too often in that shirt or because they think... (Laughter). Yes, we are glad you finally lighten up a bit here. (Laughter).

All right, so, desire is the place in which you flow emotional need into your insistence that is reality. You, as a being, you as energy, you as power, you as creativity, you as awareness and you as control, have no desire at all, none, no desire. You do not care what you experience, you only choose to experience. But, what you do not choose is ease upon this plane, you do not choose ease because it would mean that you have to be power, because it means you have to manifest upon this earth, peace, tranquility, joy, laughter and glory. For not only yourselves, but for everybody else.

You choose from the diminishment of self. If you become the power that you are, what is required of you is to live in joy, in ease, in glory.

Glory is exuberant expression of life and abundance in all things.

What is the abundance in all things? Abundance in all things is the understanding and reality that you are connected to each and every being upon this plane, to each and every molecule upon this plane and that every one of them is in support of you and the energy and power that you are. If you function as anything less than that, anything less than that, you are just being a wimp.

From that which is the debilitation of financial insecurity, you create yourself as small, as unable, and even more than that, as unwilling. Unwilling to take up the challenge of who you truly are, because you are power, you are control, you are awareness and you are creativity. And those four elements create your abundance. So, become them, use them every day for the rest of your life or until you can become them yourself. And you can add one more in there and you can say, "I am money, I am money." All right, so now we are going to ask you all to say with us, you follow with us and we are going to do some "I am's." All right? All right, so we begin:

I am power, I am awareness, I am control, I am creativity, I am money, I am control, I am power, I am awareness, I am creativity, I am power, I am awareness, I am control, I am creativity, I am money, I am awareness, I am power, I am control, I am awareness, I am power, I am control, I am money, I am creativity, I am joy. Good.

Now, feel your energy and feel the expansion that you feel of your energy. This is the truth of you and this is the place from which you create a flow of money. The tendency of each of you is to pull yourself into the small dominion that you call your body and think. Stop thinking, the brain is a useless tool for you, throw away that brain and begin to function as the truth of self, the power of you, the expansion of you. Be it in totality. Now, each of you, pull yourselves into your financial world. Does it feel good?

Student: No

R: Right, so how come you choose to live there? What limiting belief do you function from? Write that down.

What limiting belief do you function from in life that has created your financial world?

Answer: _____

Now, you remain expanded as power and look at that financial world that you have created inside of you, not as a reality, but as a space from which you function. What limiting belief do you have to have in place to function like that? Do not draw back into your bodies, we can feel you doing it. Touch the space, do not be in it. Thank you, there you go. Expand out there, yes, like that. Do not draw back into that space. You are doing it again, move out.

I am power, I am awareness, I am control, I am creativity, I am money, I am power, I am control, I am creativity, I am money, I am power, I am control, I am creativity, I am money, I am power, I am control, I am creativity, I am money, I am awareness, I am awareness, I am awareness. There, thank you.

Now, you are out of your bodies. You choose always to diminish yourself to the size of your body, then you choose a limitation about what you can receive because you think only your body receives the energy of money, which is not true. It is the lie from which you function. All right, now you are more expanded? All right, now that you have looked at that one, everybody has come up with an answer? Who does not have an answer?

S: I do not.

R: All right. You do not have an answer? So let us look. What do you consider your financial situation to be? Feel it in your body – where is it located?

S: In my eyes.

R: Your eyes? Your financial situation is here, so you cannot see what it is you are creating, eh?

S: Yes.

R: So, is awareness in your eyes? Ah, interesting, you now start to move out, notice? Yes, you start to move out. The limiting belief from which you function is, "I do not have the foresight to know what is going to happen and how to control it." True?

S: Yes.

R: Good. So how do you get yourself out of that belief? Now, have all the rest of you got your belief that you function from? Who else needs contribution here, needs to be helped?

S: I do.

R: Yes? So what is your financial situation and where do you feel it in your body?

S: In my solar plexus, and my throat.

R: Yes, all right. So, what is that solar plexus and throat? Go into it, feel it in totality, feel it, yes, there, right there. All right, you notice it is getting heavier and heavier. Yes, more and more of the financial situation that it is, which is exactly how you feel whenever you get into your financial pickle, yes? All right, so now reverse it and have it going the other direction. There, do you feel it? It is shifting now, is it now?

S: Uh huh.

R: Your financial consideration is that you have not the power or the voice to speak the truth of you, to make things happen.

S: Yeah.

R: Yes, exactly so. Good. You see. Now for each of you, you now understand the method, this is how you go about reversing the effects that you have created in your own bodies, in your own world. Where you feel your financial restrictions within your body, you reverse them and allow them to come out of you and to be outside you, not within you. To be not part of you, but as an interesting point of view, indeed. Because out here you do have a point of view, you can see it. And that which you function as, as limited by your body, you also create as limitation of your soul. Now, who is feeling dizzy? Anybody?

S: I am.

R: Slightly dizzy, here? Okay. So, slight dizzy? Why are you dizzy? Is that not where you feel considerations of money? That they sort of spin you out, you do not know exactly how to deal with them? Put that dizziness outside your head. Ah, feel that, feel that. Now you are expansion. You see it no longer a thing of being out of control in your head. There is no out of control. It is total bullshit! The only things that control you are the red lights by which you function and the green lights which tell you to go, and that is when you are driving a car. Why would you follow those green lights and those red lights when you are in your body? Pavlovian training? So, now we ask you to go back to your original questions. The first question is what?

S: What is money?

R: What is money? What is money to you? The answers.

S: My first answer was power. My second answer was mobility, third was growth.

R: Good. So which of those are true?

S: The power.

R: Really?

S: Power, it is totally true.

R: Is that really true? You think money is power? Do you have money?

S: No.

R: So, you have no power?

S: Right.

R: Is that the way you feel? Powerless? Where do you feel that powerless?

S: When you say it that way, I feel it right in my solar plexus.

R: Yes, so what do you do? Turn it out.

S: But you know, when I felt the money, I felt it in my heart, and when I have got to do something, where I feel...

R: Yes, because this is about power, the issue of power you feel in the solar plexus. You have sold your power and given it away, you must reverse that flow. Power is yours, you are power. You do not create power, you are it. Feel, there? As you turn it out, you start once again to expand, do not get into your head, do not think about it, feel it! Yes, there, you push that power out.

Now, what does that mean? For all of you, the reality is that when you have money as a power and you feel it pulling in, you are trying to create power, and as such, you have already assumed that you have none, the basic assumption. Anything that sticks your attention has the truth with a lie attached.

S: Can you say that again, please?

R: Anything that sticks your attention, about power?

S: Yes.

R: When you feel power as coming in to you, you have already assumed that you have none. You have assumed. What does that do for you? It diminishes you. Do not create from assumption, the assumption that money is power-feel it. Money as power – is that a solidity or is that only an interesting point of view? You make it so, if money is power, feel the energy of it. That is solid, is it not? Can you function as energy as solidity? No, because that is the place from which you make the box that you live in and that is where you are all trapped, right now! In the idea that money is power. Your next answer?

S: My next answer was mobility.

R: Mobility?

S: Yes.

R: Money allows you to move, eh?

S: Yes.

R: Really? You have no money but you managed to get from Pennsylvania to New York.

S: Well, if you put it that way....

R: Did you?

S: Yes.

R: And how much energy did you get here that has changed you?

S: Oh, a lot more than it took to get here. Is that what you mean?

R: Yes, it is an interesting point of view, is it not? So which way are you flowing, more out or more in?

S: Oh, from that point of view, more in.

R: Right. But you see, you always think that you are diminishing yourself because you get energy, but you do not see money as energy also, that can come in, can come in. You allow energy with great joy, do you not?

S: Yes.

R: Great gusto?

S: Yes.

R: Glory, as it were. Now, feel that glory of the energy, the energy that you have experienced the last couple of days. Feel that?

S: Yes.

R: Turn it all into money. Whoa, what a whirlwind that would be, hey?

S: (Laughter).

R: So, how come you do not allow that to be in your life the rest of the time? Because you are not willing to let yourself receive. Because the assumption is that you need. What does need feel like?

S: It does not feel good.

R: Feels like a solidity, eh? That is the lid on your box. *Need*, that is one of the dirtiest words in your language. Throw it away! Take it, right now, write it down on a piece of paper, on a separate sheet. Write "need"! Rip it out of your book and rip it up! Now you have to put the pieces in your pocket, otherwise D (another student) will have a problem. (Laughter) Good! How does that feel?

S: Good.

R: Feels great, hey? Yes, all right, so every time you use the word *need,* you write it down and tear it up until it is erased from your vocabulary.

S: May I ask you a question?

R: Yes, there are questions?

S: Yes, just about... I thought earlier that you were explaining that the words *power, energy* and *awareness* were interchangeable.

R: Not quite. If you make them significant, you have made them a solidity. You must keep them as energy flows. Power is energy, awareness is energy, as knowing with absolute certainty, no doubt, no reservation. If you think, "I am going to have a million dollars next week," and inside you hear a little voice that goes, "You want to make a bet?" or that one that says, "How are you going to do that?" or "Oh, my God, I can't believe I made that kind of commitment!" you have already counter-intended yourself to the point where it cannot occur in the time sequence you have created for it, which is the issue of control.

If you say, "I wish to have a million dollars in the bank," and you know you are going to do that and you do not put time in there, because you have the control to monitor your thought processes and each time you have a thought that is counter intention to it, you think, "Oh, interesting point of view," and erase it, it can happen very much quicker. Each time you have a thought that you do not erase, you lengthen the time period until it can't exist.

You chip away from it. You see, if you look at it from a foundation purpose, let us say that you have this golf tee, all right, and the point is here and you are going to put your idea for a million dollars on top of the point, every time you say something, you think something negative about what you have decided to create, you chip away the foundation until it tips over and falls away. And then it no longer exists. And then you build it again and you decide it again, but you have once again started to chip away continuously. The balance of it, on the point - you must get the point and keep it there as a knowing, as a reality, that it is already in existence. And that eventually, in your sequence of time, you will catch up to what you have created. Only then do you get it, do you have it, is it yours. All right, we go back to your number two answer, mobility. What is mobility? Moving your body around?

S: Well, I meant it that way.

R: You meant it as moving the body around or you meant it as freedom?

S: Well, both.

R: Both?

S: Yeah.

R: Well, once again, the assumption is that you do not have it. Notice, it is your assumptions which are the negative points of view that do not allow you, *do not allow you*, to receive what you desire in life. If you say I need or desire freedom, you have automatically created the point of view that you have no freedom. That is neither power nor awareness nor control nor creativity. Well, it is creativity of a sort. You have created it and you have made it a reality from which you are functioning. Consciousness is the process by which you will create your life, not by assumption. You can't function at assumption, a little alliteration there, time to write a poem of our own. All right. Now, your third answer.

S: The third one, oh, well, growth.

R: Oh, you have not grown in the last 20 years?

S: Well, growth, I had this idea that I need to travel to …

R: What did you say?

S: I would like to be able to travel …

R: What did you say?

S: I said, I would like, oh, I said, "I need."

R: Yes, write it down, tear it up. (Laughter). You better make smaller pieces of paper.

S: Yeah, I guess so. Yeah, I would like to be able to travel around when I hear about exciting workshops where I can learn something.

R: Interesting point of view. Now, what is the automatic point of view, the assumption, from which you are functioning? "That I can't afford it." "That I do not have enough money." Feel your energy. Feel your energy, what does it feel like?

S: It feels very expanded right now.

R: Good. But when you say that, what does it feel like?

S: When I say that?

R: Yes. When you assume that you do not have enough money.

S: Oh, that feels diminished, that feels ...

R: Good. So, do you have to function from that place anymore?

S: Hopefully not.

R: Hopefully not? Interesting point of view.

S: It sure is.

R: Consciousness, consciousness, every time you feel like that, wake up!!

When you feel like that, you are no longer being true to yourself. You are no longer being power, awareness, control, creativity or money. All right. So, anybody have any points of view about what money is for them, that they would like to have some clarification about their assumed point of view?

S: Yes.

R: Yes?

S: My first one was cosmic fuel.

R: Cosmic fuel? Is this what you truly believe and what is the assumption behind it? That you have no cosmic fuel? The assumption behind is you have no cosmic fuel. That you are not connected to the cosmos and that you are not awareness. Are any of those things true?

S: No.

R: No, they are not. So, do not function from the assumption, function from the reality. You have cosmic fuel, plenty, plenty, abundance. Yes, like that. You got it? You have another point of view you wish to ask?

S: Yes, I had a cushion for survival.

R: Ah, very interesting point of view, we would guess there are about six or seven others who might have that similar point of view. Now, what is the assumption from which you are functioning there? There are actually three in that particular point of view. Look at them, what do you see, what are you assuming there? Number one is that you are assuming that you will survive or that you must survive. How many billions of years old are you?

S: Six.

R: At least. So you have already been surviving six billion, how many of those lifetimes have you been able to take your cushion with you? (Laughter) What?

S: All of them.

R: You have taken the cushion of money with you on all of those lifetimes, the cushion of survival?

S: Yes.

R: When you speak of survival you are talking about your body, you are assuming that you are a body and that only with money can it survive. Stop breathing and breathe energy into your solar plexus, do not suck in a big bunch of air to do it. Notice that you can take in three or four breaths of energy before you feel you have to breathe and your body feels energized. Yes, like that. Now you can breathe, breathe in energy as you breathe in air. That is how you become energy and money, you breathe in energy with every breath you take, you breathe in money with every breath you take; there is no difference between you and money. All right. You get that now? Does that explain it?

S: Do I get that?

R: Do you understand now how one is functioning and what you have as an assumption there?

S: Yeah.

R: All right, and do you need that any more?

S: No.

R: Good. So, what can you do with it? Change it, you can all change those things, take away the assumption and create a new point of view as power, as energy, as control, as creativity, as money. What new point of view would you have?

S: That I am power, that I am energy.

R: Exactly so and you are, are you not? And have you always been? What an interesting point of view. All right, so, the next question, who would wish to volunteer for that?

S: You said there were three assumptions with his cushion.

R: Yes.

S: We only got one, didn't we?

R: You got two.

S: Two? Must survive.

R: I will survive, I must survive, I can't survive.

S: Okay.

R: And what is the third one? Think about it. I am unwilling to survive. The unspoken point of view.

CHAPTER TWO

What does money mean to you?

Rasputin: Read the second question please, and the answers.

Student: What does money mean to you?

R: What is your first answer?

S: Security.

R: Security, how is money security?

S: If you have it, you are securing your present and your future.

R: Interesting point of view. Is it true, is it real? If you have your money in the bank and it goes belly up, are you secure? If you have your money in a house and it burns down on the day you forgot to make the insurance payment, do you have security?

S: No.

R: There is only one security that you have and it is not money that creates it. The security is in the truth of you as a being, a soul, as one of light. And from there you create. You are power, as energy. As power, as energy you have the only true security that there is. If you lived in California, you would know there is no security because under your feet everything moves. But here, on the East Coast, you consider the ground to be secure, but it is not. That which you call the world is not a solid place, it is but energy. Are these walls solid? Even your scientists say no, that the molecules move only more slowly, that is why they appear to be solid.

Are you solid? Secure? No, you are space between a bunch of molecules that you have created and formed to the apparency of solidity. Is that a security? If you could be secure with money, could you take it with you when you die? Could you manage to get a new body and come back and get it next lifetime? So, is it really security that you buy with money, does it really mean security, or is that only a point of view that you have taken on, that you have bought from another, as to how you create your life?

S: So, what you are telling me is that if I think money, I can create it?

R: Yes. Not if you think it but, if you BE it!

S: How do I become money?

R: First of all, you must have the vision of your life, and you do that by "I am creativity." You are creativity as a vision. You are "I am power," as energy. You are "I am awareness," as knowing exactly that the world will be as you see it. And you are "I am control," not in a vested interest in how you get there, but in the awareness that the universe will move the cogs to bring about your vision if you maintain your power and you maintain your awareness in alignment with what you do. Then, if you have those four elements in place, you can become "I am money."

And you can use these, you can say, "I am power, I am awareness, I am control, I am creativity, I am money." And use them every morning and every night until you become money, until you become creativity, until you become awareness, until you become control, until you become power. That is how you become money. The "I am" of being it. Because it is that, that is how you create yourself now. You see, if you are creating yourself from the point of view of "I am getting security by getting money," what is that? It is a time sequence, a futurity, yes?

S: Right.

R: So you can never achieve it.

S: Do you always have to be in the present?

R: Yes! "I am" puts you always in the present. So, what other point of view do you have about money, what it means for you?

S: Well, security was my main, because the other two would be home and future. But, if I had security, my home would be secure and my future would be secure. So it is really on …

R: Really? Is that really true?

S: No, no, no, it is not. I understand what you just brought me through as my first need for security.

R: Yes, good.

S: I understand the "I am's."

R: Yes. Anybody else have a point of view that they wish some clarity on?

S: Happiness.

R: Happiness, money buys you happiness, eh?

S: I think so.

R: Really, do you have money in your pocket?

S: Not much.

R: Are you happy?

S: Uh, huh.

R: So, money did not buy you that, did it?

S: No.

R: That is right, you create happiness, you create the joy in your life, not money. Money does not buy happiness, but if you have the point of view that money does buy happiness, and if you do not have money, how can you have happiness? And the judgment that comes in after that is, "I do not have enough money to be happy." And even when you get more, you still do not have enough money to be happy. You get the point? How do you feel about it?

S: I just, like I am always happy even though I do not have money, but knowing I have someone to pay on Thursday, knowing I do not have any money, tends to put me in a worse mood.

R: Ah, there we go, now we are getting into it – time. How do you create money?

S: With a job, by working.

R: That is an interesting point of view. You mean you can only receive by working?

S: That is what I have experienced.

R: So, which point of view came first, the idea that you had to work to get money or the experience?

S: The idea.

R: Right. You have created it, have you not?

S: Yes.

R: So, you are responsible for it; you have created your world exactly as your thought pattern is. Throw your brains away, they get in the way of you! You think, you do not grow rich, you grow limited. You get that thought process in the way and then you are diminished, you have limited yourself on what you are going to achieve and what you are going to get. You have always been able to create happiness, have you not?

S: Yes.

R: It is only the bills that get in the way, yes?

S: Yes.

R: Because what you do is, you think, you have a vision of money, of what your life will be like yes?

S: Yes.

R: So, get a vision of that now. How does it feel? Light or heavy?

S: Light.

R: And when you are in this lightness, do you know that you will pay everything that you owe?

S: Will you say that again?

R: In this lightness, do you know, as awareness, that you will always pay everything you owe?

S: Yes.

R: You know it? You have absolute awareness and certainty of it?

S: That I have to pay everybody I owe.

R: No, not that you have to, but that you will.

S: Yeah, I think I will.

R: Oh, interesting point of view, I think I will. If you are thinking that you will pay it, do you have the desire to pay it or, do you resist it?

S: I resist it.

R: Yes, you resist it. Yes, you resist paying? What is the purpose of resisting?

S: I could not tell you.

R: What would be the underlying point of view of not desiring to pay? If you had enough money, would you pay the bill?

S: Yes.

R: So, what is your underlying point of view that is unexpressed?

S: That I am worried about money, that I do not want to pay.

R: That you will not have enough, yes?

S: Yes.

R: Yes, it is the unexpressed point of view, it is what you cannot look at that gets you in trouble. Because that is a place you have created from, from the point of view that there is not enough, at all. So, have you created that as reality, that there is not enough?

S: Yes.

R: Is this a place you like to function from?

S: I do not understand what you are saying.

R: Do you like to function from "not enough"?

S: Yeah.

R: So what is the value of choosing "not enough"?

S: There is not any.

R: There must be or you would not make that choice.

S: Don't we all have that fear?

R: Yes, you all have that fear that there will not be enough, and you all function from the certainty that there will not be enough, which is why you are looking for security and why you are looking for happiness and why you are looking for homes and why you are looking for future, when, in reality, you have created every future you have ever had. Every past, every present and every future is created by you. And you have done an impeccable job of creating it exactly as you think it. If you think there is not enough, what are you creating?

S: Not enough.

R: Exactly so, there is not going to be enough. Now, congratulate yourselves on such a good job, you have done an impeccably wonderful job of creating "not enough." Congratulations, you are very good, you are great and glorious creators.

S: Creating nothing.

R: Oh, now, you have created something, you have created debt, have you not?

S: All right, this is right.

R: You have been very good at creating debt, you have been very good at creating "not enough," you have been very good at creating sufficient to feed yourselves and clothe yourselves, yes? So you have done an excellent job of all that part of create. So, what point of view is it that you are not creating from? No limitation, no limitation.

S: Doesn't that take a lot of practice?

R: No, it takes no practice.

S: Really, do we just do it constantly?

R: Yes, all you have to do is BE "I am creativity," the vision of your life. What would you like your life to look like? What would it be if you could create it any way you chose? Would you be a millionaire or would you be pauper?

S: Millionaire.

R: How do you know it is better to be a millionaire than a pauper? If you are a millionaire somebody might come along and steal all your money, if you are a pauper nobody would come and steal your money. So, you would wish to be a millionaire? For what purpose? Why would you wish to be a millionaire? What value is there in being a millionaire? Seems like a good idea, but it only seems like a good idea, right?

S: Yeah, it is a good idea.

R: It is a good idea, ok. All right. So let us have a little fun here. Close your eyes, get a vision of a hundred dollar bill in your hand. Now tear it up into little pieces and throw it away. Ooh, that hurt.

Class (Laughter).

R: Get a vision of a thousand dollars, now tear that up and throw it away. That hurt more, didn't it?

S: Yes.

R: Now, ten thousand dollars and burn it up, throw it in the fireplace. Interesting, it was not as hard to throw ten thousand dollars in the fireplace, was it? All right, now throw a hundred thousand dollars in the fireplace. Now throw a million dollars in the fireplace. Now throw ten million dollars in the fireplace. Now BE ten million dollars. What is the difference between ten million dollars in the fireplace and being ten million dollars?

S: It feels much better.

R: Good, so how come you always throw all your money in the fireplace?

Class: (Laughter)

R: You are always throwing your money away and you are always spending it as a way to try to be happy, as a way to try and survive. You do not allow yourself to create so much that you feel that you are money, that you are willing to be money. Willingness to be money is to be a million dollars or to be ten million dollars. To be it, it is only energy, it has no real significance unless you make it so. If you make it significant, you make it heavy. If it is significant, it becomes a solidity and then you have trapped yourself. The box of your world is the parameters by which you create your limitation. Just because you have a bigger box does not mean it is less a box, it is still a box. You get the point.

S: Yes.

R: You like the point?

S: Yes.

R: Good.

S: It is still difficult. (Laughter)

R: Now that is an interesting point of view, it is difficult to be money, heh?

S: Yes.

R: Now, look at that point of view. What are you creating with that point of view?

S: I know; I am limiting stuff.

R: Yes, you are making it difficult, solid and real. Boy, did you do a good job on that. Congratulations, you are a great and glorious creator.

S: Those two magic words, I am.

R: I am money, I am power, I am creativity, I am control, I am awareness. All right, anybody else have a point of view that they would like explained more?

S: You can make it without working for it?

R: You can make it without working for it. Now there are two very interesting limitations. First of all, how do you make money, you have a printing press in your back yard?

S: No.

R: And without working for it, what is work to you?

S: A paycheck.

R: Work is a paycheck?

S: Yes.

R: So, you sit at home and collect one of those?

S: No, I go to work.

R: No, work for you is something you hate to do. Feel the word *work*, feel it. How does it feel? Does it feel light and airy?

S: No.

R: Feels like shit, heh? (Laughter) Work, is it work to look in your crystal ball.

S: No.

R: Well, no wonder you do not make any money. You do not see what you are doing as work, do you?

S: I do not know what I am really doing yet.

R: Interesting point of view. How can you be "I am awareness" and not know what you are doing? What is the underlying assumption there? What is the underlying point of view from which you are functioning? It is "I am afraid'?

S: No, I do not understand.

R: You do not understand what? If you doubt your ability, you can't change. Yes?

S: It is not that I doubt it. It is that I do not understand it. I do not know what I am seeing.

R: Good, so turn loose of your mind, connect with your guides and let the ball guide you. You are trying to think it through and figure it out from your point of view of thought. You are not a thinking machine; you are psychic. A psychic does not do anything but be there for the images to come and to turn loose of their mind and turn loose of their mouth and let it flow. Can you do that?

S: Yeah, I do that.

R: And you do it very well when you let it happen. It is only when you put your mind into the equation that you create disability. The unfortunate part for you is that you do not trust what you know. You do not recognize that you, as the unlimited being that you are, have access to all the knowledge in the universe. And that you are but a pipeline for the awakening of cosmic consciousness. The reality is that you live in fear … the fear of success, the fear of your power and the fear of your ability. And, for each of you, underneath your fear is anger, intense anger and rage. And who are you outraged at? Yourself. You are angry at yourself for picking and choosing to be the limited beings that you are, to not walk in the tallness of the God Force that you are, but to function from the limited size of your body as though it is the shell of existence. Expand yourself out and move away from it by being not afraid and not in anger, but in the great and glorious wonder of your ability to create. Creativity is vision. Do you have visions?

S: Yes.

R: Knowing, as awareness, knowing is the certainty that you are connected to the power of you. Do you have that?

S: Yes.

R: And control, are you willing to turn it over to the cosmic forces?

S: If I learn how.

R: You do not have to learn how; you have to be "I am control." That which you see outside of you, you cannot have. "Learning how" is the way in which you create debilitation and you put into your computation of achievement the value of time as though it really exists. You know everything that will be in the future and you know everything that has been in the past, right now. There is no time but that which you create. If you would move yourself, you must move yourself from the point of view of "I am control" in the surrendering of the need to figure out how to get from Point A to Point B, which is "if I learn." That is going from Point A to Point B. You are trying to control the process and the destiny of self from diminishment. You can't achieve it from there. You understand?

S: Yes.

R: Are you willing to look at your anger?

S: Yes.

R: So look at it. How does it feel?

S: Wrong.

R: And where do you feel it, in what part of your body?

S: In my chest.

R: So take it now and push it three feet in front of you, from your chest. Push it out. Good. How does it feel now? Heavy or light?

S: It does not feel very heavy.

R: But it is three feet away from you, yes? Now, that is your anger, is it real?

S: Yes.

R: It is? Interesting point of view. It is only an interesting point of view; it is not a reality. You have created it, you are the creator of all your emotions, you are the creator of all of your life, you are the creator of everything that occurs for you. You create, and if you must put time in the computation, then put time in ten second increments. All right, we are going to give you a choice here. You have ten seconds to live the rest of your life or you are going to be eaten by a tiger. What do you choose?

S: (no reply)

R: Your time is up; your life is over. You have ten seconds to live the rest of your life, what do you choose? To be a seer or not? You did not choose, your life is over. You have ten seconds to live the rest of your life, what do you choose?

S: To be.

R: Yes, to be, choose something. As you choose, so do you create your life, so choose to be the psychic that you are, choose to be the reader of the crystal ball, in ten second increments. If you have to look into your ball now and you look into it and you get a picture in this ten seconds, can you answer what it is?

S: Yes.

R: Right, you can. Now that lifetime is over, you have ten seconds of life, what are you going to choose? The picture and the ball and the talking or no choice?

S: The picture and the ball.

R: Good, so choose it, choose it each and every time. Every ten seconds you choose anew, choose anew, get yourself going. You create your life in ten second increments. If you create it in anything other than ten second increments, you are creating from the expectation of the future, which never arrives, or from the debilitation of the past based on your experience, with the idea that it is going to create something new when you maintain the same point of view. Any wonder your life still shows up the same? You are choosing nothing new, are you? Moment by moment you choose "I do not have enough; I do not want to work."

Now, we are going to recommend some words for you to eliminate from your vocabulary. There are five words that you should eliminate from your vocabulary. One: the word *want*. *Want* has 27 definitions which mean "to lack." You have had thousands of years of the English language in which the word *want* means "to lack" and you have had more lifetimes of speaking English than just this one. And, in this lifetime, how many years have you used the word *want* as though you thought you were creating desire? In truth, what you have created? Want, lack; you have created lack. So, you are a great and glorious creator, congratulate yourself.

S: (Laughing).

R: Two: *need*. What is need?

S: Lack.

R: It is the debilitation of knowing you cannot have, you cannot *have* anything if you need. And need will always be followed by greed, because you will be trying to get. Three: and then we come to *try*. *Try* is never achieving, *try* is making no choice, *try* is doing nothing. Four: then we have *why*. And *why* is always the fork in the road and you will always come back to the beginning.

S: I do not see that.

R: Listen to a two-year-old some time and you will understand it.

S: (Laughter). You never get an answer.

R: Five: *But.* Whenever you say "but" you counter your first statement, "I would like to go but I can't afford it." All right, do not be need. "I need" is saying "I do not have." "I want" is saying "I lack." "I try" is saying "I do not do." "I but," you better pat yourself on the fanny, eh? Next question.

CHAPTER THREE

What three emotions do you have when you think of money?

Rasputin: All right, so who wishes to volunteer for the next question?

Student: Number three?

R: Number three. Yes. What is the question?

S: What three emotions do I have about money?

R: What three emotions, yes. What three emotions do you have about money?

S: Umm...

R: Three emotions when you think about money.

S: The first one that came up I did not like very much, but it was fear.

R: Fear? All right. So, what assumed point of view would you have to have, to have fear about money?

S: Well, I interpret it as different, um, interpret it in a different way, that I feared its absence, which...

R: Yes. That is why the emotion is there, you fear absence of it because the basic assumption is...

S: I need it.

R: Write it down.

S: And tear it up.

R: Write it down and tear it up.

S: I'm going to ask you a terrible question.

R: Okay.

S: Okay, I go to the store, they need, want, something in return for what I am going to take from them. (Laughter).

R: Want, want, what is want?

S: (Laughter)

R: They lack, yes, *want* means to lack. That is the other dirty word you must eliminate. But, what do you go to the store for?

S: Okay, food.

R: All right. So you go to the store for food, what makes you think you *need* to eat?

S: You're joking. Well, I do know I *need* to.

R: *Need*? Write it down again.

S: *Want.*

R: Write it down and throw that one away too. *Need* and *want* not allowed.

S: But you get hungry.

R: Really? Pull energy into your body, all of you, put in energy. Yes, do you feel hungry? No. Why do you not eat more energy and less food?

S: That would be very good for a while because I could lose some weight, but it'd start to hurt. (Laughter).

R: Exactly so. You get enough energy in there, you might be a giant balloon.

S: What about my friends who come over, including the two people who are sleeping in my house right now?

R: So, who said you need to feed them? How come they can't contribute to you?

S: They are.

R: The fear is that you will not receive. The fear is that money works only one direction and that is away from you. Whenever you feel fear, you create *need* and *greed*.

S: Okay.

S: *Need* is really out of fear, sir?

R: Yes, on fear, fear brings in *need* and *greed*.

S: Really?

R: Yes.

S: Holy moley, you're right. I think I just realized another thing that is a basic belief system or that it wasn't really a good thing.

R: Not a good thing to receive.

S: Not a good thing to have too much of.

R: Not a good thing to receive.

S: Right. Or, to receive from others.

R: To receive, period.

S: Right.

R: From anywhere. All right. What ... if you are in fear, you are unwilling to receive because you think that you are a bottomless pit and where you live is a deep, dark hole. Fear is always the hole in you, it is a bottomless place.

Fear makes of you need, greed, and you become an asshole in the process. All right?

S: All right.

R: Next emotion.

S: Desire for more.

R: Desire, ah, yes. Ah, yes, now desire – what is that? You go out and wiggle your hips to get more?

S: (Laughter) I knew it wasn't the greatest.

R: Desire means, and automatically you have "get more." Notice, get more, an insufficiency which goes along with fear.

S: You know, not to just get more money but …

R: Get more, period. Money has nothing to do with the reality of what you are experiencing. Money is the subject around which you create a reality of nothingness, of not enough, of *want, need, desire* and *greed*. And it is the same for everyone on this plane. It is where this world has functioned.

You have a great example of it in what you call your 80's and it has been the truth of this world since the time in which you decided, all you decided, that money was a necessity. A necessity. What is a necessity? Something that you cannot do without and survive. You, as beings, have survived millions of lifetimes and you cannot even remember how much money you had or how much money you spent or how you did it. But, you are still here and you are still surviving. And each one of you was able to come to a place to understand more about it.

Do not function from the assumption that it is a necessity, it is not a necessity, it is the breath of you, it is what you are, you are money in totality. And, when you feel yourself as money and not as necessity, not as necessity, you are expansive. And when you feel yourself as necessity, in relationship to money, you diminish self and you stop the flow of energy and money. And your third emotion?

S: Happiness.

R: Ah, now, happiness in what respect? Happiness when you spend it, happiness when you have it in your pocket, happiness when you know it is coming, happiness because it is money? Can you just look at a dollar bill and have happiness?

S: No.

R: What part of it brings happiness for you?

S: Knowing that certain things can be accomplished or done.

R: So money buys happiness?

S: Well, I used the wrong word, um....

R: How does happiness come from money?

S: It doesn't necessarily come from it at all.

R: So how do you feel happiness in relationship to money? When you have sufficiency? When you have abundance of it? When you feel security?

S: Yeah, security.

R: Security. Interesting point of view.

S: But there is no such thing as security.

R: Well, there is. There is security. There is security in knowing and having the awareness of self. That is the only security there is, the only security you can guarantee is that you will go through this lifetime and you will leave this body and you will have the opportunity, if you desire, to come back and try again to be a more abundant creature upon this world. But, happiness is within you, you have happiness, you are happiness, you do not get it from money. To be happy, it takes to be happy, that is all. And you are happy except when you choose to be sad. Right?

S: Right.

R: Anybody else have emotions they wish to speak about?

S: Well I just, I'd like to go a little more on the fear.

R: Yes.

S: Because I've spent an enormous amount of energy on the emotion fear.

R: Yes.

S: And behind fear, underneath fear, is always anger.

R: Yes, exactly so. And what are you truly angry about. Who are you angry at?

S: Myself.

R: Exactly so. And what are you angry about?

S: Feeling the emptiness.

R: Not taking your power.

S: Em, hem.

R: Not being you in totality. Feel that?

S: Very much.

R: Feel, in your body, where you fear and you anger.

S: Yes.

R: Now turn it out the other direction. Now what does it feel like?

S: Relief.

R: Yes, and that is how you get rid of fear and the anger to make space for you. Because, if you look at yourself, there is no fear in your universe at all, is there?

S: No.

R: And the only anger that you can express is towards others because your real anger is about yourself and where you have refused to take up the truth of your energy in totality. So, can you be the power that you are, the energy that you are? So let it go, stop holding it in. There, like that. Whew, relief, hey?

S: Yes.

R: Now, you have to practice this one, all right?

S: Yes.

R: Because you have diminished yourself, as have all the others in this room, continuously for billions of years, to be not self, not power. And you have done it to squash your own anger. Interesting, hey? Anger with self. And there is not one of you here who is not angry with yourself for not allowing yourselves to be in totality the power that you are. Well, that blew some stuff. All right, anybody else wish to speak about emotions?

S: I'd like to speak about fear again, from my point of view. When I get in fear it's a constriction, a closing down.

R: And where do you feel it?

S: In my solar plexus.

R: Good. So turn it out, turn it out. There, like that. What does it look like now?

S: Fearful.

R: Good. And what is underneath the fear?

S: Anger.

R: Anger. Yes, there, that thing that you have tied up in a little knot in there. You've got that well hidden, hey? You think. All right, not let the anger out, not let it out in totality. Feel the anger, let it come out of you. Yes, there, that is it. Now notice the difference and the expansion. You feel that?

S: Yeah, it does feel very good.

R: Yes, it feels very good. It is the truth of you, you are doing expansion as being exterior from your body, not having the capacity to be connected at all to this place. Feel, as you let the anger go, the reality of connecting to self in totality, not as some kind of spiritual entity, but as truth of self. There is a calmness and a peace that comes over you when you do it in truth. Let it out in totality. Like that, there.

S: I do, I got it.

R: You feel, that is the trust of who you are, that is power. The other is removal.

S: It's like, it feels like a coming into myself.

R: Exactly so. It is being totally connected, totally consciousness, totally awareness and control. How does control feel from this place?

S: It feels a lot different from the other control.

R: Yes, the other is trying to control your anger, is it not?

S: Well, I suppose.

R: Well, ultimately you are trying to control your anger because the truth is you are not allowing yourself to shine. There is peace, there is calmness and there is magnificence inside. But you cram it in underneath anger. Since you think your anger is not appropriate, you diminish yourself. And you try to control it and you can try to control everything else around you, as a way of hiding it from yourself. Who you are angry with is self. Be at peace with self. There, right there. Do you feel that?

S: Right.

R: Yes, that is it. And that is you. Feel your energy expanding.

S: Oh, it's so different.

R: Extremely. Yes, that is it, dynamically you, that is who you truly are. All right.

S: And it is blackness and I think I have some control on it and I ...

R: All right.

S: I also know that I have some out of control on it at this point.

R: So where do you feel the blackness?

S: I seem to think that I go into it rather than it into me, I'm not sure of that.

R: Where do you feel it? Is it outside of you? Is it in you? Close your eyes, feel the blackness. Where do you feel it?

S: I think in my lower stomach area and then I let it engulf.

R: Good. So how do you think to feel? It is in your mind …

S: Okay, the works.

R: … that you are experiencing the blackness? And what it is, is the sense that there is nothing except blackness connected to money. And that somehow that blackness has to do with evil and, therefore, the receiving of it is absolutely not allowed. There, you feel that shift? Turn it, yes there. Turn it white, there, feel your crown opening. Yes, and now that which you call the blackness can pour out. And that which is the reality of you is present. Notice the difference in your energy. You have let go of the idea, the emotion of evil as a reality, because it is not reality. It is only an interesting point of view. All right? Any other emotions?

S: I think my dominant emotion about money is ambivalence.

R: Ambivalence? Ambivalence, yes. What is ambivalence? Where do you feel it?

S: I feel it in my solar plexus and in my lower chakras.

R: Yes, Ambivalence is about the unknowing of this plane. A sense that money belongs to something that you do not understand. You feel that shift in your lower chakras?

S: Yes.

R: That is the result of connecting to the fact that you are awareness, and as awareness, you are money, as awareness, you are also power and all chakras are connected unto energy, which is you. There, does ambivalence still exist for you?

S: No.

R: Good. All right, any other emotions?

S: I've got one.

R: Yes.

S: I feel distaste and shame.

R: Very good emotions, distaste and shame. Where do you feel that?

S: I think I feel it ...

R: You think feelings?

S: No. In my stomach and my lungs.

R: In your stomach and your lungs. So, for you money is breathing and eating. Shame, turn it out, move it out of your stomach. Yes, you feel that, you feel the energy of your stomach chakra now opening?

S: Yes.

R: Good. And what is your other emotion?

S: Distaste.

R: Distaste. In your lungs. Distaste because it means you must suffocate to get it. You must suffocate yourself to get money from your point of view. Is that a reality?

S: Yes.

R: It is?

S: No, no, no.

R: All right.

S: I recognize it as a being ...

R: How you are functioning?

S: Yes.

R: Good. So turn that breath and exhale all of it. Good, now breathe in money. Good, and exhale shame. And inhale money through every pore of your body and exhale distaste. Yes, now how does that feel, little freer?

S: Yes.

R: Good. Anybody else wish to speak about emotion?

S: Fear.

R: Fear, what other emotions?

S: Anxiety and relief.

R: Money gives you relief?

S: Yes.

R: When?

S: When it comes to me.

R: Um, interesting point of view. Anxiety and fear, let us take those first because they are the same. Where do you feel fear and anxiety? In which part of your body?

S: My stomach.

R: Stomach. All right, push that out from your stomach, three feet out in front of you. What does it look like to you?

S: Slimy and green.

R: Slimy?

S: Yeah.

R: Yes. What is the reason that it is slimy and green?

S: Because I can't control it.

R: Ah, interesting point of view, no control. You see you are not being "I am control," are you? You are saying to yourself, "I can't control, I am not in control." That is the underlying assumption from which you function. "I am not in control; I am not control." So, have you created, very well, fear and anxiety.

S: Yes.

R: Good, you are a great and glorious creator, well done! Do you congratulate yourself on your creativity?

S: With shame, yes.

R: Ah, interesting point of view. Why with shame?

S: Because I didn't know any better.

R: Yes, but it doesn't matter whether you knew better. What does matter is that you now understand that you are creator and you have done a magnificent job of creating, which means you can choose differently and you can create a different result.

S: It takes discipline.

R: Discipline? No.

S: With luck.

R: No, with power! You are energy as power, "I am power, I am awareness, I am creativity, I am control, I am money." All right? That is how you create change, by becoming the "I am" that you are instead of the "I am" that you have been. Begin to look at where you have created the viewpoint of solidity around money and what it feels like. When you feel it impacted upon a body part, push it out from you and ask yourself, "What is the underlying point of view that I am functioning from that I do not even see?" And allow yourself to have the answer. And then, allow that the answer is just an interesting point of view after all, anyway.

And what can I choose now? I choose "I am creativity, I am awareness, I am control, I am power, I am money." If you create "I am not," if you create "I can't," you will not be able to. Also, congratulate yourself on what you have created and do it with great and glorious gusto. And there is nothing wrong with what you have created except your own judgment of it. If you were a bag lady on the street, would that be a better creation or a worse creation than what you currently have?

S: Worse.

R: Interesting point of view.

S: Not if you didn't know.

R: That is right, not if you didn't know. Now you know that you have the choice, you can create. Now, what happens if your next-door neighbor tells you that you are not getting paid this week because "I am taking all your money to pay for the fence you have busted"?

S: An interesting point of view.

R: Exactly, it is an interesting point of view. That is all it is. If you become resistance or reaction to it, you make it a solidity and then your neighbor will take the money.

S: So, what you are telling us is that when somebody comes up with the negative …

R: With any point of view about money.

S: All right, that's an interesting point of view.

R: Yes, feel your energy when you do that.

S: Okay, and then go right into the "I am's"?

R: Yes.

S: I got it. The light has dawned.

R: And when you feel impacted on your body, a particular point of view, an anxiety or a fear, what is that about?

S: That you have to take it out and push it away from you.

R: Yes. And when you feel anxiety and fear in your stomach, are you talking about not being fed amply?

S: No.

R: Are you talking about not being nurtured? So, what are you talking about? Body is what you are talking about. You feel money as a function of your body as though it is a third dimensional reality. Is money a third dimensional reality?

S: No.

R: No, it is not, yet you try to make it so. Look at your points of view about money, it is security, it is house, it is bills, it is food, it is shelter, it is clothes. Is that true?

S: Well, that is what you buy with it.

R: That is what you buy with it, but you do that by choice, do you not?

S: Oh, necessity.

R: That is what you are choosing in that ten seconds. Necessity, huh? Interesting point of view. Do you choose your clothes that you wear by necessity?

S: Yes.

R: You do?

S: Yes, I do.

R: You don't choose them because they are pretty or because they make you look good?

S: Most of the time they are to keep me warm.

R: And what about in the summer, when you wear a bikini?

S: Cool, and then I am looking good. (Laughter).

R: Right, so you make choices, not a necessity but what you wish to feel, yes? Feel?

S: Yeah, but, you do need...

R: But! Throw that word away.

S: Yikes. (Laughter). You do have to have shoes and you still have ...

R: How come you have to have shoes; you can walk barefoot.

S: Maybe I can but ...

R: Sure you can.

S: I need them, it is cold out there.

R: Need, huh?

S: Underwear and socks ...

R: Need, huh?

S: You have to have.

R: Who said? How do you know you can't talk to your body and ask it to make yourself warmer?

S: Then what about...

R: You, as a being, do not even need the body?

S: Well, that would be cool.

R: That is cool.

Class: (Laughter).

R: Yes?

S: Well, you have to have food, you wear shoes.

R: We do not wear anything. Gary wears shoes but that is because he is a wimp, he will not walk in the snow without them.

Class: (Laughter).

R: He thinks it is cold.

S: It is, too.

R: Well, that is an interesting point of view. You should try Siberia if you want cold.

S: And your children, when they are hungry?

R: How many times have you had your children hungry?

S: Couple of times.

R: And how long did they go hungry?

S: For the night.

R: And what did you do?

S: Got money from my father.

R: You created, did you not?

S: Yes.

R: Did you congratulate yourself upon your creative ability?

S: Well, I thanked my father.

R: Well, that is one way to create. Creating, creativity, is being the awareness of self. Be "I am creativity," be "I am awareness," be "I am power," be "I am control," be "I am money." You are resisting; *"but," "need," "why," "you must," "it's a necessity,"* are all points of view of *"I can't have"* and *"I don't deserve."* These are the underlying places that you are functioning from. Those are the points of view that are creating your life. Is this where you wish to create from?

S: Well, I can see that in every aspect but money.

R: Yes, but money because you see money as different. What do you see money as – the root of all evil?

S: Yeah.

R: Whose point of view is that? In truth, it is not your own, it is one you bought. The devil made me do it, heh? You see, it is a reality that you are creating it as different, as not part of your creativity.

S: So if you say to yourself all of the "I am's," it is going to put money in my pocket?

R: It's going to start to come in your pocket. Every time you doubt, you chip away at the foundation that you are creating. Let us put it this way, how many times have you said, "I want money"?

S: Every day.

R: Every day. I want money. You are saying, "I lack money." What have you created?

S: But it is true.

R: That's true? No, it is only an interesting point of view. You have created exactly what you have said: I want money. Now, you did it unconsciously, but you did create.

S: Well, how about if I wanted to hit the lottery?

R: If you "lacked" hitting the lottery, that is exactly what you would create – lack of hitting the lottery.

S: The power of perception is what we are saying.

R: The power of your words, of your awareness, creates the reality of your world. You want a simple exercise? Say "I don't want money."

S: Can we choose something else instead?

R: Say "I don't want money."

S: I don't want money.

R: Say "I don't want money."

S: I don't want money.

R: Say "I don't want money."

S: I don't want money.

R: Say "I don't want money."

S: I don't want money. That sounds negative to me.

R: Really? "I don't lack money" is negative?

S: But, we do want money.

R: You don't want money!

R: That is right. "I don't want money." Feel the energy of it, feel how you feel as you say, "I don't want money." *Want* means to lack, you keep trying to hold on to the definition. I am money. You can't be "I have money," you can't have something you are not being. You are already being creativity as "I want money" and so you have created an abundance of lack, have you not?

S: Yes.

R: Good, so can you say now, "I don't want money"?

S: I don't want money (Repeated many times).

R: Now, feel your energy, you are lighter. So, feel that?

S: Yes, I am dizzy.

R: You are dizzy because what you have created is a breaking down of the structure of reality as you have created it. You all have it; say it to yourselves and feel that you get lighter and more laughter in your life as you say, "I don't want money."

S: Can you say, "I am rich"?

R: No!! What is rich?

S: Happiness.

R: Really? You think Donald Trump is happy?

S: No, not money rich.

S: Oh, like money controls what we have to.

R: That is an interesting point of view, where did you get that one?

S: Because ...

R: Where did you get that point of view?

S: I got that idea from thinking the ...

R: See, it is that thinking thing, you get in trouble. (Laughter). Did it feel good?

S: No.

R: No, it doesn't feel good, it is not true. If you say "I am rich," does it feel good?

S: It would feel good.

R: Oh, interesting point of view – it would feel good? How do you know, have you been rich?

S: Well, I had money when I …

R: Have you been rich?

S: No.

R: No. Can you be rich?

S: Yes.

R: Really? How can you be rich when you can say only "If I was"? You see, you are looking at the future and an expectation of it and what it should be, not what it is.

S: It's, it's, like you have a boss that is going to pay you and you have to do what he says and you have to …

R: Do you have a boss that is paying you?

S: Not at the moment but …

R: That is not true, you have a boss that is paying you and, she is not paying you very well because she is not taking any money for what she can do. You are it, honey! You are your boss. Create your business, create your life and allow it to come to you. You are sticking yourself in the closet and saying, "I can't, I can't, I can't." Who is creating that point of view? What happens if you say, "I can and I understand," instead of, "I can't and I don't understand"? What happens to your energy? Feel your energy.

S: I am just stuck in the point where the kids can't eat without money.

R: Who said you would be without money? You did, you assumed you would have no money unless you did something that you hate. How often do you look at work as fun?

S: Never.

R: That is the point of view; that is the underlying point of view. And yet, you say, my work is working with the crystal ball. So you never see yourself as having fun. Do you love what you do?

S: Yes.

R: So how come, if you do what you love, you can't allow yourself to receive?

S: I don't know enough yet; I need more information.

R: You do not need more information; you have at your disposal ten thousand lifetimes of being a crystal ball reader. Now what have you got to say about learning, besides, oh, shit?

Class: (Laughter).

R: Busted, busted, you don't have any place to go now to hide.

S: So, I read what I saw in the ball and it was inaccurate and I felt like an asshole.

R: Yes. (Laughter) How do you know it would be inaccurate?

S: Well...

R: Well?

S: I don't know.

R: So, will they come back again?

S: I don't know.

R: And when you do it for the next person and you do it right, will they come back again?

S: Yes, I'd have to say yes.

R: So, how come you say you don't know already? Who are you lying to?

S: What?

R: Who are you lying to?

S: It's it's …

R: Who are you lying to? Who are you lying to?

S: I swear to you; I don't know what I'm seeing.

R: That is not true, that is not true. How come you have customers who come back to you who think…

S: I got it right.

R: Yes, you got it right. What makes you think you are not getting it right all the time? How many customers do you have who do not come back to you?

S: None.

R: Boy, now this is a hard case, she takes a lot of convincing, doesn't she? She is definitely going to make sure that she has no money and no abundance and no prosperity in her life. Interesting boss you have. Not only do you not pay yourself well, you don't even acknowledge yourself as having enough business. Since, to know that you are doing well, you have created customers who come back again and again. You know how many customers it would take, in increase, to give you abundance in your life?

S: Maybe thirty more a week.

R: Good, so can you allow thirty more a week to come into your space?

S: Yes, no problem.

R: No problem?

S: No problem.

R: You sure?

S: Yes, I am positive on that.

R: Good, so can you allow yourself to have a hundred thousand dollars? A million dollars?

S: Yes.

R: Ten million dollars?

S: Yes.

R: Good, you shifted a little bit now, thank you very much, we are all appreciative. You are a creator, a great and glorious creator. Congratulate yourself on every time you complete a reading that you love. And do your work from love, be not work, be fun. You are having fun with what you do, you are not having work. Work feels like shit, fun is fun, and you can do it forever. You create what it is, no one else. You can pump gas and have fun, you can wash windows and have fun, you can clean toilets and have fun. And you will get paid for it and you will have a great and glorious prosperity. But, only if you are having fun with it. If you see it as work, you have already created it as something you hate. Because that is what this plane is all about: work is hardship, difficulty and pain. Interesting point of view, hey?

S: What if you don't know what you want to do?

R: But you do.

S: I do, but before, I didn't know before I got led to it.

R: And how did you get led to the ball? You allowed yourself to connect intuition and sight and you asked the cosmos to match your vision and to give you what you desired. You created, as vision, you had the power of your being, the knowing, as awareness, the certainty that it would occur and the control to allow the universe to provide for you. So, you have, already, the four elements to be "I am money." Got it?

CHAPTER FOUR

What does money feel like to you?

Rasputin: Good. So the next question, who wishes to volunteer for the next question?

Student: I will.

R: Yes. What is the next question?

S: What does money feel like to you?

R: What does it feel like, yes that is correct.

S: Then that's different than the emotions you feel about money?

R: Well, not necessarily.

S: I said, "Oh, great."

R: So what does money feel like to you?

S: Right now it feels very confused.

R: Is like confused. Do you feel that money, that confusion, is an emotion?

S: An emotion and a thought.

R: It is a state of mind, yes.

S: Yes.

R: So, remember when we spoke about that which was the dizziness?

S: Yes.

R: Did you open your crown chakra and allow it to move out? Confusion is a created image of money. What assumption would you have to have to have confusion? You would have to assume that you do not know. The assumption would be "I do not know and I should know."

S: That is why I feel confused.

R: That is right. I do not know, I should know. These are opposing points of view which create confusion and they are only interesting points of view. Feel that shift when you say that about each one of them? I should know, I don't know. Interesting point of view, I don't know. Interesting point of view, I should know. Interesting point of view, I don't know. Interesting point of view, I should know. How does the confusion feel now?

S: Well, except for the fact that I...

R: Of course.

S: For me, right now, it seems very unreal in the sense that the perspectives for me are money and energy, power and creativeness, in their purity, that seems very clear when I'm not dealing with money, where I don't have to have some.

R: What is the assumption from which you are functioning?

S: That there is some reality not understood.

R: Exactly so.

S: That is the real problem.

R: That is not the problem, that is the assumption from which you function, which says to you automatically, that it is different from the reality of you. Your assumption is that physical reality is not the same as spiritual reality, as the reality of who you truly are. That purity does not exist upon this plane, that you can never bring that purity unto this plane.

S: That's right.

R: Those are assumptions; those are false information from which you have created your reality.

S: Well, it's also confused by the fact that there seem to be other beings that have different realities and that there isn't any confusion for other people, it seems. The people themselves, the viewpoints of other people, the people on my street, the people at the store...

R: And what is it about that, that you are speaking of? That there are other realities? That other people have different realities? Yes, there are some ...

S: From a different point of view and that ...

R: Is there anybody here who does not identify with what she has said? They all have the same point of view you do.

S: You mean they are all confused?

R: Yes. They all think that you cannot bring to reality, that which is the spiritual world, into the physical reality, and every man on the street has exactly the same point of view. And only those who do not buy that point of view, who do not assume that it is absolutely impossible, are able to create and even they are only able to create in small ways, their reality.

If you focus your life upon making money and your sole goal in life is to be Donald Trump, Bill Gates, that does not matter, same image. Same person, different body, same person. Their life is about making money, everything they do is about money. Why do they have to make so much money? Because, like you, they are sure they are going to run out of it next week.

S: It's not just a game for them?

R: No, it is not just a game for them, they are functioning from the point of view that there is not enough and they will never have enough, no matter what they do. It's just a different standard, that is all.

S: You are saying these people do not feel a certain freedom from their fortunes?

R: You think Donald Trump has freedom?

S: To some extent, I think so.

R: Really? He is able to drive in a limousine, does that give him freedom or does that mean he has to have body guards to safety him from everybody around him, who are trying to take money from him? Does it give him freedom to have 27 people who are trying to get money out of him every day?

S: It gives the illusion of freedom.

R: No. It gives you the illusion that this is freedom. You only think it is freedom because you do not have it. He is no freer than you, he just has more money to spend on things that he does not need. You think it makes him a bigger spirit because he has more money?

S: No, surely not.

R: Does it make him a lesser spirit?

S: No.

R: Oh, interesting point of view there you guys got. (Laughter). You were all thinking it, you just didn't have the nerve to say it, "Well, that makes him worse because he has more money."

S: Yeah, you're right.

R: Yes, that is what you were thinking, you did not say it but you thought it.

S: Well, that makes some people control everything around him.

R: Really? Yes, he is controlling, he is controlling the sun, the moon, the stars, he has total control of those things.

S: But controlling people are not...

R: Oh, controlling people, so that is your standard of greatness.

S: That's not my standard, no, no, no. That's not my standard. We're talking about Gates and his acquisitions and Trump and his acquisitions, to determine his control.

R: Is he being control, in truth?

S: No. I ...

R: Or is he controlled by his need for money? His life is totally boxed in by the necessity of creating more and more and more and more money. Because that is the only way that he feels adequate.

S: But I also think that he, the energy he puts out to absorb ...

R: All right, you have another word that you are going to personally put into your vocabularly to eliminate.

S: What?

R: But.

S: But?

R: But. Every time somebody tells you something, you get a 'but' out (Laughter).

S: This is true for ...

R: It is true for many of you, for most of you, that when you are given a piece of information, you instantly start to create an opposite point of view, because it does not align or agree with you. Because it does not align or agree, because it is resistance on your part to allow it to be or because you are in reaction to it. After all, it is only an interesting point of view that this man is run by money.

S: That is what I wanted to say but I ...

R: No, you have another point of view, as an interesting point of view, that is all it is.

S: Yes, I'm learning that.

R: It is of no value. Every time you create a consideration about money, you create a limitation upon yourself. Upon yourself! And every time you tell somebody else what your point of view is, you create a limitation upon them. You wish to create freedom? Then Be freedom. Freedom is no consideration at all!!

What would the world look like if you manifested all of life with ease and joy and glory, with no consideration about limitation at all? If you had unlimited thought and unlimited ability and unlimited allowance, would there be graffiti, would there be homeless, would there be war, would there be devastation would there be blizzards?

S: So, what's the difference, wouldn't there be weather?

R: If you had no consideration about blizzards, there would be weather, there would not have to be snow storms. Listen to your television set, when it comes close to the time when there is going to be snow coming to you, yes, they manifest, they go talking about how great a storm it is going to be. The storm of '96, the second storm of '96, is going to be a great and glorious blizzard here and it is going to be devastation and you better get to the store and buy more right away. How many of you buy that point of view and start to create your life from it?

S: Not the buying, I could spend the afternoon in the park.

R: You bought the point of view, that is what we are talking about. You instantly decided it was true. Do not listen to your television sets, get rid of them. Or watch only those programs that are totally brainless. (Laughter) Watch "Scooby Doo." (Laughter) Watch cartoons, more interesting point of view on them. You listen to the news, you're going to be very depressed and you're going to have many ideas about what money is.

All right so where were we? Okay let us go back here. Confusion, you understand about the confusion now?

S: No.

R: All right. What more would you wish to understand here? You are creating the confusion.

S: Who am I? Am I a body? Are you here? Is there someone else here?

Is there a reality? Is there any difference? What the hell is existence? Are you, or is everything, pure energy and there's no separation between spirit and soul and consciousness, that this is it, is it, is it, is it? There's nothing to be said about anything, so all the suffering and all the sorrow and all the illusion and all the separation and all of the confusion, well, what is that? What?

R: Creation.

S: Right.

R: You have created...

S: So on this level we create something that humans, which is a creation, and this ego self which is a creation, considers that there's something called money and location, which is a creation which means that if we're on Wall Street or we're doing the US history of 1996 of New York City, then we are agreeing that you and these other people co-exist together. I don't understand this.

R: Why do you not understand?

S: Everybody else is you and you are everybody else.

S: That's something... I don't understand it.

R: You are creating yourself as separate, you are creating yourself as different, you are creating yourself as debilitated and you are creating yourself as anger.

S: I'm so frustrated.

R: Yes, but it's really anger underneath.

S: Oh, yes.

R: Because you feel powerless, that is the basic assumption from which you are functioning, and that is always the basic assumption of confusion. Every confusion is based on the idea that you have no power and you have no ability.

S: But I don't.

R: You do.

S: I feel I don't.

R: Look at your life, look at your life, what have you created. Did you start out with a magnificent amount of money? Did you start out with a palace and lose it all? Or did you create and create and then get into confusion about it and get into doubt about it and get into feeling powerless to do or to know how to control it and then it began to fall away from you because you were creating confusion and you were creating doubt about yourself?

Yes, that is where your life went, but none of it is the truth of you. You, as a being, have total power to create your life and you can and you will and it will come together in more magnificent ways than you can even imagine. But it will come from you having faith, and this is for all of you. Faith in yourself, faith in knowing that you have created the reality that exists now and the awareness that you are willing to change it. That you do not desire to be that any longer. That is all it takes, the willingness to allow it to be different.

S: So if life changes, does that mean that it's confused consciousness that creates more Bosnia's and homeless people? Where does that consciousness go, where do the dark entities that I may have created, or that some other portion of me that's been so separated from views that's on the television set which I see or the homeless person, where does that go if I say, "Well, it's not in my reality, I don't believe in it, I don't choose that anymore."

R: It's not a matter, you see you are doing that from resistance.

S: Right.

R: Right? For change to occur you must function in allowance, not resistance, not reaction, not alignment or agreement. Allowance is...

S: I'm willing to allow it, I just want to understand where...

R: You are functioning at resistance because you are trying to understand from something that does not really exist. That other people, in their own free will and choice, are also creating from something that does not exist, a continuation of acceptance, alignment or agreement, reaction or resistance.

Those are the functional elements of your world; you, in order to change it, must function at allowance. And every time that you are in allowance, you change all of those around you. Every time somebody comes at you with a strong point of view and you can say, "Ah, interesting point of view," and be in allowance of it, you have shifted the consciousness of the world because you have not bought it, you have not made it more solid, you have not gone into agreement with it, you have not resisted it, you have not reacted to it, you have not made it reality. You have allowed reality to shift and change. Only allowance creates change. You must allow yourself as much as you allow others, otherwise you have bought the store and you are paying for it with your credit cards.

S: So does that become total pacification for the world?

R: Absolutely not. Let us do this, all of you think about this for a minute. But S, you be the guinea pig here, okay? All right. You have ten seconds left to live the rest of your life, what are you going to choose? Your life is up; you did not make a choice. You have ten seconds to live the rest of your life, what do you choose?

S: I choose not to choose.

R: You are choosing not to choose, but you see, you can choose anything. If you begin to realize that you only have ten seconds to create from, ten seconds is all it takes to create reality. Ten seconds, less than that in trust, but for right now, that is the increment from which you must function. If you function from ten seconds, would you choose joy or sadness?

S: I'd have to take sadness.

R: Exactly so. You see, you have created your reality from the choice of sadness. And when you choose from the past or you choose from the expectation of the future, you have not made any choice at all, you have not lived and you are not living your life, you are existing as a monumental, monolithic limitation. Interesting point of view, hey?

S: Yes.

R: All right, so what is your next answer? Number two on your list of what you... What was the question, we've forgotten.

S: What does money feel like to you?

R: What does money feel like to you, yes, thanks.

S: To me the bottom line, I guess, on this plane, is fight in prison...

R: Ah, yes. Very interesting point of view, hey? Money feels like fight in prison. Well, that certainly describes everybody in this room. Is there anybody who does not see that as the reality of what they've created?

S: Fight in prison?

R: Yes.

S: I don't.

R: You don't see that?

S: A little bit. I don't understand what that means, actually.

R: You are not fighting constantly to get money?

S: Oh, all right.

R: And you do not feel it is a prison that you do not have enough?

S: I give up (Laughter).

R: Fine.

S: We all must be in a similar reality.

R: You're all living the same reality. So, do we need to make even a comment about this?

S: Yeah. What about S, with his barter system?

R: Well, is that not a small prison of it's own?

S: I don't know for sure, how do you feel about it, S?

S: Yes, it is.

R: Yes, it is. You see, everybody has their own point of view. You are looking at S and seeing his reality as freedom but, he is looking at Donald Trump as freedom. (Laughter).

S: Okay, you're saying do we have to talk about it, well, how does this kind of go with it?

R: Allowance. Interesting point of view, hey? That I feel imprisoned by money, that it feels like prison to me. Does it feel like velvet to you? Does it feel like expansion to you? No. It feels like diminishment. Is that a reality or what you have chosen and how you have chosen to create your life? It is how you have chosen to create your life. It is not more a reality than the walls. But you have decided that they are solid and they keep the cold out. And, so, they work. So, also, do you make your limitations about money, with the same sort of solidity. Begin to function in allowance, that is your ticket to get out of the trap that you have created. All right? Next question.

CHAPTER FIVE

What does money look like to you?

Rasputin: All right, next question, what does money look like to you?

S: Green and gold and silver.

R: So, it has color, it has conformity, it has solidity. Is that the truth of it?

S: No.

R: No, money is just energy, that is all it is. The form that it takes in the physical universe, you have made as a significance and a solidity and around it so you create a solidity of your own world which creates a disability to have it. If it is only gold or silver that you see, then you better have lots of chains around your neck. If it is green, if you wear green clothes, do you have money?

S: No.

R: No. So it is that you must see money, not as a form, but as an awareness of energy because this is the lightness from which you can create the totality of it in abundance.

S: How do you see energy?

R: Just as you felt it when you pulled it into every pore of your body; that is how you see energy. You see energy with the feeling of awareness. All right?

S: Yes.

R: Next question.

CHAPTER SIX

What does money taste like to you?

Rasputin: Now, the next question. What is the next question?

Student: What does it taste like?

R: Good. Who wishes to answer that one? This should be fun.

S: Money tastes like rich, dark chocolate.

R: Emm, interesting point of view, hey? (Laughter)

S: Paper, ink and dirt.

R: Paper, ink and dirt, interesting point of view.

S: Dirty blindfold.

S: My taste buds on the side of my mouth start to salivate.

R: Yes.

S: Sweet and watery.

S: Slippery filth and barn marbles and peach trees.

R: Good. All right. So, it tastes very interesting to you people, hey? Notice that money tastes more interesting to you than it feels. It has more variation in it. Why do you think that is? Because you have created it as your bodily function. For S, money is about eating, eating chocolate, yes. Yes, you see everybody has a point of view about how money tastes like something. It's slippery, interesting, goes across your tongue easily, em? Does it go down easily?

S: No.

R: Interesting point of view. Why does it not go down easily?

S: It sticks.

R: Interesting point of view: hard, chunky, crunchy. Really interesting points of view you have about money.

S: But it's all the same point of view.

R: It's all the same point of view, it is about the body.

S: Even though it seems different, she's...

R: Even though it seems different.

S: ...she said chocolate and I said bitter, but that's the same.

R: That is the same, it is about body; it has to do with your body.

S: The tasting does.

R: Really?

S: Yes.

R: You cannot have taste out of the body?

S: Not on an English sandwich.

R: But money, the point of it, was that money is a function that you see as a bodily function. You see it as a third dimensional reality not as a reality of creation. You see it as something, as solid and real and substantial, as something that has taste and form and structure. And, therefore, it has a particular kind of attitude that goes with it. But, if it is energy, it is lightness and ease. If it is body, it is heavy and significant, and heavy and significant is where you have created it, is it not?

S: Yes.

R: Is that not where all your viewpoints come from?

S: So, as you asked about taste we went into assumptions again.

R: Assumptions. You instantly assumed that it was body, that it is where you live, it is how you function. You know, it is slippery, it is dirty, it is all kinds of things, it is germ ridden. What an interesting point of view about money.

S: Sometimes, it's warm and cool.

R: Warm and cool? Is it really that?

S: There's like another one, it has this trust factor behind it that you hold this, a gold standard like...

R: That is a point of view, a consideration that you bought. Is it a reality? Not any more!! (Laughter) Is there anything behind money? Pick up a dollar bill, what do you see behind it?

S: Air.

R: Nothing, air! Lots of air, that is all that is behind it (Laughter).

S: A lot of hot air.

R: A lot of hot air, exactly so. (Laughter). And when you listen to people talking about money, do they create it as hot air, do they speak of it as hot air? Yes, but how do they create it? It is very significant and heavy and massy, is it not? Weighs on you like a ton of bricks. Is that reality? Is that how you wish to create it for yourselves? Good. So, begin to look at it, feel it. Feel, every time you hear a consideration come at you about money. This is your homework part along with all the other of this. Every time you feel the energy of some consideration, idea, belief, decision or attitude about money, feel where it hits you in your body. Feel the weight of it and turn it to light. Turn it to light, it is only an interesting point of view.

It is only an interesting point of view; that is all it is; it is not a reality. But very quickly you'll begin to see how your life has been creating, the money flows in it, from your very will, participation in buying everybody else's point of view. Where are you in that configuration? You have gone, you have diminished yourself, you have let yourself disappear and you have become a lackey, a slave, to that which you call money. It is no more a truth than the air that you breathe is truth. It is no more significant than taking a breath. And it's no more significant than seeing the flowers. Flowers bring you joy. Right? You look at flowers; it brings you joy. When you look at money, what do you get? Depressed, there is not as much there as I wished for. Never do you give gratitude for the money you have, do you?

S: No.

R: You get a hundred dollars you go, "Oh, this will pay a bill, damn it, I wish I had more." (Laughter). Instead of going, "Whoa, did I manifest something good or not?" You do not celebrate what you create, you go, "Oops, didn't make enough again." What does that say? How does that manifest in your life? If you look at the bill, if you find a dollar bill on the ground, you pick it up and you put it in your pocket and think, "Oh, I'm lucky today." Do you think, "Boy, did I do a great job of manifesting, did I do a great job of creating some money flows for me"? No, because it wasn't ten thousand dollars, which is what you think you need. That *need* word again.

S: What does money taste like?

R: What does it taste like?

S: Dirty.

R: Dirty? No wonder you don't have any money. (Laughter).

S: Sweet.

R: Sweet. You have more money.

S: Good.

R: Good, tastes good, you get a little money in your stocking as well.

S: Like water.

R: Like water, goes pretty quick, like water, huh? (Laughter). Right through the bladder. What other points of view? No others, nobody else has any other points of view about money?

S: Yucky.

R: Yucky. When was the last time you tasted money?

S: As a kid.

R: Right, because you were told as a little child that it was dirty, don't put it in your mouth. Because you bought the point of view that money was yucky. You bought the point of view that it was not goodness and that it was not energy, but that it was something to be shunned. Because it was dirty, because it did not provide for you as a goodness. And you bought that very young and you have retained that point of view forever. Can you choose different now?

S: Yes.

R: Good. Allow yourself to have the reality that it is only an interesting point of view. Whatever money tastes like. It is not a solidity, it is an energy and, you are energy too. All right? Have you created your world around the points of view of money that you have? Is it dirty, is it yucky, do you have limited amounts of it because you don't wish to be a dirty person? Sometimes it is more fun to be dirty, it was in my lifetime. (Laughter).

CHAPTER SEVEN

When you see money coming toward you, from which direction do you feel it coming?

Rasputin: All right. So now, the next question. What is the next question?

Student: What direction do you see money coming from?

R: Good. What direction do you see money coming from?

S: In front.

R: Front. It's always in the future, eh? You are going to have it some time in the future, you're going to be very rich. We all know that.

S: But sometimes I see it coming out of nowhere.

R: Out of nowhere is a better place, but nowhere, where is nowhere? Out of anywhere is a better place to have it coming from.

S: How about everywhere but up?

R: Well, why are you limiting it?

S: I know, I never thought of that.

R: Never thought it was okay for rain to come as...

S: No, rain I saw, but I didn't think it was coming up from the ground. Your own money tree.

R: Yes, let money grow everywhere for you. Money can come from anywhere; money is always there. Now, feel the energy in this room.

You are starting to create as money. You feel the difference in your energies?

Class: Yes.

R: Yes, where do you see it coming from?

S: My husband.

Class: (Laughter).

R: My husband, others, where else?

S: Career.

R: Career, hard work. What points of view are you talking about, here? If you are looking for it from some other person, where is that person located? In front of you, beside you, behind you?

S: Behind me.

R: If it's your ex-husband.

S: It is.

R: Yes, so you are looking to the past, from him, to get your life. Is that where you create from?

S: No, but I think...

R: Yes, all right. You're lying. So, first of all, take all the places that are in this room and draw energy from this room, in through the front of you, through every pore of your body, pull it in through every pore of your body. Good, and now, pull it in from the back of you, through every pore of your body. Good. And now, pull it in from the sides of you, through every pore of your body. And now pull it in from the bottom of you, through every pore of your body. And now pull it in from the top of you, through every pore of your body. And now you have energy coming in from everywhere and, money is but another form of energy and turn it into money now, coming in through every pore of you from every direction.

Notice how you made it more solid, most of you. Make it light, make it energy again that you are receiving. And now make it money. Good, that is better, that is how you become money, you flow it in through every pore of your body. Do not see it coming from other people, you do not see it coming from other space, you do not see it coming from work; you allow it to flow in. And now stop the flow from every part of your body. And now we wish you to flow energy out of the front of you, as much as you can. Flow it out, flow it out, flow it out. Is your energy diminishing? No, it is not. Feel, at the back of you, energy is coming in as you flow it out the front.

There's no end to energy, it continues to flow; as does money. Now, pull energy into every pore of your body, from every place. Good, right there. And now, notice that as you are pulling it from everywhere, it is also going out from everywhere, it is not a stagnant. Now, turn it into money and you will begin to see money flying around, everywhere around you. Yes, it goes in and out and around and through. It continues to move; it is energy – like you. It is you, you are it. There, like that.

All right, now, stop the flowing. Now, flow money, hundreds of dollars of money to anybody else in the room, in front of you. Flow it out, massive amounts of money, see them gaining massive amounts of money, flow it out, flow it out, flow it out, flow it out. Notice, you are still pulling energy in the back and, if you allow, as much energy will come in the back as you flow out the front and you are still doing it as money. This give you an idea? When you think that you have not enough money to pay a bill and it is a hardship to flow out the money, it is because you have closed down the backside of you and you are not willing to receive it. Money flows in as it flows out, when you block it by your point of view that there will not be enough tomorrow, you have created a disability in yourself. And you have no disability but the ones you personally create. All right, everybody got that? Next question.

CHAPTER EIGHT

In relationship to money, do you feel you have more than you need or less than you need?

Rasputin: All right. Next question.

Student: In relationship to money, how do I feel, "I have more than I need or less than I need?"

R: Yes. In relationship to money do you feel you have more than you need or less than you need?

S: Less.

S: I'd have to say less.

S: Everybody said less.

R: Yes, well that is a given, hey? There is not one of you who thinks you have enough. And because you always see it as need, what are you always going to create? Need, not enough.

S: But, how about paying the bills tomorrow?

R: Yes, you see, you're always looking about how you're going to pay the bill tomorrow, exactly so, thank you very much. It's always about how you're going to pay that thing tomorrow. Today do you have enough? Yes!

S: I'm okay?

R: "I'm okay," who is saying that? Interesting point of view you have there, I'm okay. I am great, I am glorious and you create more now.

My money is wondrous, I love this much money, I can have as much as I desire. Allow it to come in. Be grateful for the fact that you have it today, do not worry about tomorrow, tomorrow is a new day, you manifest new things. Opportunities come to you, right?

Now, the mantra: "All of life comes to me with ease and joy and glory." (Class repeats the mantra several times). Good, now feel that energy, is it not the same as "I am power, I am awareness, I am control, I am creativity, I am money"?

S: And love?

R: And love. But you are always love, you have always been love and you always will be love, that is a given.

S: Why is it?

R: Why is it a given? How do you think you created yourself in the first place? From love. You came into this place with love. The only person you do not give love to with ease is yourself. Be that loving to yourself and you are money and you are joy and you are ease.

CHAPTER NINE

In relationship to money, when you close your eyes, what color is it and how many dimensions does it have?

Rasputin: In relationship to money, when you close your eyes, what color is it? And how many dimensions does it have? Anybody...

Student: Three dimensions.

R: Blue and three dimensions, hey.

S: Multi-dimensional?

S: Green and two.

S: Green and three.

R: Interesting, that it is only two dimensions for the most of you. A few of you have multi-dimensional. Some of you have three.

S: I had wide open space.

R: Wide open space is a little bit better. Wide open space is where money should be, feel the energy of that. Then money can come from anywhere, can it not? And it is everywhere. When you see money as wide open space, there is no scarcity, is there? There is no diminishment of it, it has no form, it has no structure, it has no significance.

S: And no color?

R: And no color. Because, all right, you are looking at United States dollars, how about gold? Is that green and have three sides? No. And how about silver? Well, that is sort of iridescent sometimes, but even that is not enough. And is it liquid? You have liquid colors?

S: No.

R: What about the man in the store? Well, in what way would you wish to speak to him? You are going to the store to buy? What assumption...

S: It's expensive.

R: Yes, it is wide open spaces, but you, we are talking about allowing yourself to have so much money come into you that you never think about it. Never think about money. When you go to the store do you look at the prices of each and every item you buy and add it all up to see how much, to see if you have enough money to spend?

S: Sometimes I'm afraid to open my credit card statements.

R: Exactly. Do not open those credit card statements if you do not wish to know how much money you owe. (Laughter) Because you know you have not enough money to pay them. Automatically you have assumed that.

S: I just don't want to look at it.

R: Don't want?

S: To look at it.

R: Write it, write it down.

S: Want, want, want.

R: Want, want. Write it down, rip it up. No more *want*, no more *need*, not allowed. Okay?

CHAPTER TEN

In relationship to money, what is easier, inflow or outflow?

Rasputin: All right. Now, next question.

Student: In relationship to money, what is easier, inflow or outflow?

R: Is there one person here who said inflow is easier?

S: If they did they lie. (Laughter) I know I didn't.

R: Right, considering the fact that you do not look at your credit card debts, it definitely was not the truth.

S: I'm not sure which.

R: I'm not sure, interesting point of view, hey? All right. So, for all of you, the idea that money flows out is most often the most significant point of view that you hold on to. It is so easy to spend money, it is so hard to work, I have to work hard to make my money. Interesting point of view, hey? Now, who is creating those points of view? You are!!

So, feel money, feel energy coming into your body. All right, it's coming in from everywhere, feel it coming in. All right, now flow energy out the front of you, feel it coming in the back and allow it to be equal. Now, feel hundreds of dollars going out the front of you and hundreds of dollars coming in the back of you. Good. Feel thousands of dollars going out the front of you and thousands of dollars coming in the back of you. Notice how most of you got a little solid on that one. Lighten up, it is just money, it is not significant and you do not even have to put it out of your pocket at this point. Now, let millions of dollars flow out the front of you and millions of dollars' flow in the back. Notice it is more easy to flow millions of dollars than it is to flow thousands of dollars. Because you have created a significance about how much money you can have, and when you get to millions there is no more significance left.

S: Why?

R: Because you don't think you are going to have a million, so it is irrelevant. (Laughter).

S: Well, I had more trouble letting money come in the back, maybe I think I'm going to.

R: Maybe, but you are definitely more willing to let your money flow out than you are willing to let it flow in. That is another interesting point of view, hey? Now, energy out equals energy in? Yes, of sorts. But there is no limitation to energy and there is no limitation to money except those you yourself, create. You are in charge of your life, you create it and you create it by your choices and your unconscious thoughts, your assumed points of view that oppose you. And you do it from the place of thinking that you are no power, that you have no power and that you cannot be the energy that you are.

CHAPTER ELEVEN

What are your three worst problems with money?

Rasputin: Now, what is the next question?

Student: What are your three worst problems with money?

R: Oh, this is a good one. Who wishes to volunteer for that one?

S: I will.

R: All right, over here, yes.

S: I am very fearful of not having any money.

R: Ah yes, well, we have talked about fear, okay? So, do we need to cover that more? Everybody pretty clear about that now? Okay, next.

S: I want to buy lots of things.

R: Ah, interesting point of view, buying lots of things. What do you get by buying lots of things? (Laughter). Lots to do, lots to take care of, you fill up your life with lots of things. How light do you feel?

S: Burdened and then I find myself giving them away, to neighbors, birthdays...

R: Yes. So what is the value of buying lots of things?

S: It's in my blood.

R: So, how come that is one of your considerations?

S: Because it bothers me.

R: It bothers you that you buy?

S: Yes.

R: Good. So, how do you overcome the desire to buy? By being power, by being awareness, by being control and by being creativity. And as you come to the place in which you feel you need to buy, the reason you are buying is because you assume you have not enough energy. Bring energy into you. If you wish to break the buying habit give money to the homeless person on the street or send it to a charity or give it to a friend. Because what you have done is you have decided that you have too much money coming in. And so you must make sure that you equalize the flow from your point of view. You see how you are doing that?

S: Yes. Yeah, I actually do have too much inflow.

R: Yes. So, can there be too much inflow as opposed to outflow? No, it is a created reality. And what you are existing there and what you are assuming, is that you are not spiritual, you are not connected to your god force, if you have too much of it. It does not matter, in truth, what does matter is the choices you make about how you create your life. If you create as energy, if you create as power, if you create as awareness and you create as control you will have joy in your life, which is what you are trying to achieve in the first place. Ease and joy and glory, this is what you desire, this is what you are after and this is where you are going. And this is what you will all achieve if you follow the directions we have given you this night. All right. Now, have we covered all the questions?

S: Just, the same thing, if I have the money and I feel like, well, somebody else doesn't have this and so I should give it to them. And, so then I don't have as much, or I worry about it.

R: So what if you give them energy?

S: Give them energy instead of giving money?

R: Yes, it is the same.

S: So when the guy's begging in the subway, you just... (Laughter)

R: Well, you have just...

S: They ask for a dollar and you just...

R: Have you not breathed in energy here tonight?

S: Yes.

R: Have you not eaten your fill of energy? What is the purpose of eating? To get energy. What is the purpose of money? To have energy. What is the purpose of breathing? To have energy. There is not difference at all.

S: It sure seems different.

R: Only because you decide and create it as different. The assumption is that it is a difference.

S: That's right.

R: And when you assume that, you start creating from that position which creates lack of money and lack of energy.

S: But it's, it just doesn't seem quite right to me, because it seems that part of what I'm assuming is that I am a human being, that...

R: Well, that is a bad assumption right there.

S: Well, I'm living in a human society with such creations as bread, water, time, government...

R: So you are creating yourself as a body.

S: I'm creating myself as S in 1996, New York City, yes.

R: You are creating yourself as a body. Is that where you truly wish to be? Are you happy there?

S: Well...

R: No!

S: When I was out of the body there were other places that seemed much worse, so this seemed like a good stopping point to see how I could solve that problem. Meanwhile it was pretty bad new ...

R: Right. But you are creating the realities in whichever place you are, by your own point of view.

S: It doesn't seem that way to me, it seems that others create with me or for me, on top of me. I don't think I could totally say that, I don't think so, maybe, but I don't think so.

R: You don't control what we say?

S: What you say. I mean, you and I are connected somehow...

R: Yes.

S: ... and everyone is, but... and... the paradox is that you are you and I don't wonder about this, you are a spiritual being.

R: And so are you.

S: And you are S (another student), and you are S (another student), and we are sharing some reality here together, we are in New York in 1996, are we not? But I'm in with you somehow, I don't think that I'm you.

R: That is right, that is what we have been talking about, you don't think. Every time you think...

S: I have a problem.

R: You have a problem.

S: You got it. (Laughter).

R: So throw it away, your brain, it is a useless piece of debris.

S: And just jump off the roof.

R: And jump off the roof and start to float as the being that you are. You, when you throw away your brain and stop the thought process, every thought has an electrical component to it, which creates your reality. Every time you think, "I am this," "I am a body," that is exactly what you become. You are not S, you are an apparency of S at this time, but you have been millions of other lives and millions of other identities. And you still are being those, right now. Your consciousness, the greatest portion of it from your point of view, is right here, right now. That, also, is not a reality. When you disconnect from the thought that your reality is created in this moment with your total consciousness and start to see where you have got other ideas, other points of view and other people's attitudes, beliefs, decisions and ideas, you will start to connect to those other dimensions that can give you greater reality upon this plane than anything you are trying to create right now from your thought process. And that is where you truly desire to go.

Thinking gets in the way of living because it is not a creative process, it is a trap. Next question.

CHAPTER TWELVE

Which do you have more of, money or debts?

Rasputin: Next question.

Student: Which do you have more of, money or debts?

R: Which do you have more of?

S: Debts

S: Debts.

R: Debts, debts, debts, debts. Interesting, everybody has debts, why is that? Why is it that you have debts? Feel the word *debt*.

S: Oh, it's heavy.

S: Yes.

R: It feels like a ton of bricks. So, we give you a little hint, how to lighten it up. Because it sits in such heaviness upon you that you buy the point of view that it is the most significant of things about you, is it not? Because it is heavy, because it is significant, because it is solid – you add to it, you add to it, because you buy the idea that it is okay to go in debt, you buy the idea that one should be in debt and you buy the idea that you can't have enough money, anyway, without doing it. Is that real?

S: Uh, huh.

R: Interesting point of view. It is real?

S: Yeah, that's what I used to think.

R: Good, well, do you think that anymore?

S: No.

R: Good. All right, so how do you get rid of your bills and your debts? By paying off past expenditures. Can you make past expenditures into a solidity? Feel it, does it feel like debt?

S: No judgment on it.

R: No judgment, exactly. And yet you judge yourself, significantly, on your debt, do you not? And, when you judge yourself, who is it that is kicking you?

S: Myself.

R: Right. So, why are you angry at yourself for creating debt? Well, you should be. You are great and glorious creator of debt, you are a creator, you have created magnificent debt, have you not?

S: Oh, yes.

R: Very magnificent debt, boy, am I good at creating debt! All right, so see the glorious creator that you are as debt. Be the glorious creator that you are to pay off your past expenditures. Feel the lightness in past expenditures - that is how you create a shift in your consciousness. Lightness is the tool, as you are light, as you are being light as money, you create a shift and a change in your consciousness and everybody around you. And you create a dynamic energy that starts to shift the totality of the area that you live in and the place and how you receive money and how it comes in to you and how everything in your life works. But, know that you are a great and glorious creator and that everything that you have created in the past is exactly what you said it was, and what you create in the future will be exactly what you create it to be, by the choices you make. All right, next question.

CHAPTER THIRTEEN

In relationship to money, to have an abundance of money in your life, what three things would be a solution to your current financial situation?

Rasputin: All right, so we have two more questions. Yes?

Student: One more question.

R: One more question. What is the last question here?

S: In relationship to money, to have an abundance of money in your life, what three things would be a solution to your current financial situation?

R: Good. So who wishes to volunteer for this one?

S: I do.

R: All right.

S: Do what I love and do best.

R: Do what I love and do best?

S: Yes.

R: So, what makes you think you cannot do what you love and do best? And what is the basic assumption there?

S: That I lack money to get there.

R: Well, what do you love to do best?

S: I love to garden and do healing.

R: Gardening and healing? And are you doing those things?

S: Sometimes.

R: So what makes you think you are not getting what you desire?

S: Um…

R: Because you are spending seven days a week doing something you hate?

S: Exactly.

R: Who created this reality?

S: But, well…

R: They do not have need of gardeners around this city? How come you did not become a gardener if you love to garden?

S: Because I'm in the process of doing, making that happen, but I…

R: So what is the basic underlying assumption from which you are functioning? Time.

S: Time, yes.

R: Yes, time.

S: There hasn't been time to create.

R: Yes. There hasn't been time to create. What did we speak about in the beginning? Creativity, creating the vision. Power, being I am power, you are giving the energy to what you desire, awareness of the knowing that you will have it. Where do you continually undermine your knowing that you will have what you desire? You do it every day when you go to work and you say, "I still have not got it."

S: That's right.

R: What are you creating from the point of view? Still never having it and tomorrow you will not have it either because you still have the point of view that you have not got it. And you have taken the matter of control and you've decided there must be a particular path that is necessary to travel to get there. If the path to getting you there is that you have to be fired to take it on, you don't know, do you? But, if you decide that the only way you can do it is to keep this job that you hate, because that will give you the freedom to get where you wish to go, you have created a delineation and a path, a way that you must get there, which does not allow the abundant universe to provide for your way.

Now, we are going to give you another little statement which you shall write out and put up some place where you see it on a daily basis. Here we go:

I allow the abundant universe to provide me with a multiplicity of opportunities all designed to encompass and support my growth, my awareness and my joyful expression of life.

This is your goal; this is where you are going.

R: All right. S, what is the next answer you have?

S: Be out of debt so I can catch up with myself and be free.

R: Be out of debt. What is the basic underlying assumption there? That I will never be out of debt and that I am in debt. So what are you saying to yourself everyday? "I am in debt, I am in debt, I am in debt, I am in debt, I am in debt, I am in debt, I am in debt." How many of you are in debt?

S: We all are, probably.

R: And how many of you say that with great abundance and diligence? (Laughter).

S: Not me.

S: Diligence. (Laughter).

R: Good, so do not create from there. Create from "I am money." Do not worry about what you call your debt, pay on it a little bit at a time. You wish to pay it off instantly; take 10% of everything that comes in and put it on your debts. And do not call them debts at all. Listen to the sounds of *debts*. Sounds really good, hey? Call it past expenditures. (Laughter).

S: I'll do!

S: That's great, that is really great.

R: Hard to say, "I am past expenditures," is it not? (Laughter). Hard to say, "I am in past expenditures." But, "I am paying off past expenditures is easy." See how you get out of debt? We also must not ignore the freedom aspect there. The underlying point of view is that you have no freedom, which means you have no power, which means you have no choice. Is that really true?

S: No.

R: No. You have chosen your experience, every experience in your life, every experience of your life has been about what? Creating greater and greater awareness within you. Nothing you have chosen in the past was for any other purpose than awakening you to the reality and the truth of yourself or you would not be here this night. All right?

S: Could you repeat that again?

R: Nothing you have done or chosen in your life has been for any other purpose than to awaken you to the truth of yourself or you would not be here this night. How about that, we did it word for word? (Laughter). All right. So, your next point of view?

S: To live a simpler life.

R: What a crock of shit that is. (Laughter).

S: I know. (Laughter). I knew it even when I was writing it. (Laughter)

R: There is not one of you who desires a simpler life, simpler life is very easy – you die! Then you have a simple life. (Laughter) Death is simple; life, life is an abundance of experience. Life is abundance of everything, life is an abundance of joy, an abundance of ease, abundance of glory, it is the reality and the truth of you. You are energy unlimited, you are in totality everything that this world is made of and each time that you choose to be money, to be awareness, to be control, to be power, to be creativity, you change this physical plane into a place in which people can truly live with absolute awareness, absolute joy and absolute abundance. Not just you, but every other being upon this plane is affected by the choices you make. Because you are them, and they are you. And as you lighten up your own considerations, as you do not pass on and stick others with your considerations, you create a lighter planet, a more awakened and aware civilization. And that which you desire, that which you have wished for, that which is the place of peace and joy will come to fruition. But you are the creators of it, be in the knowing of it, be in the joy of it and maintain it.

Now, once again we reiterate, your tools,

- When you feel the energy of thoughts about money coming in on you and you feel them pushing in, reverse them and make them go out of you until you can feel the space that is you once again. And then you will know that they are not you and that you have created that reality.

- Remember that you create the vision of what you will have by connecting the power, the energy to it. And by being aware that it is a reality that is already in existence because you have thought it. You do not have to control how it gets there, you are control and therefore it will occur as quickly as the abundant universe can provide it for you. And it will, do not judge.

- Be in gratitude every day for each thing that you manifest, when you get a dollar, be in gratitude, when you get five hundred dollars, be in gratitude, when you get five thousand dollars, be in gratitude and that which you call your debts as past expenditures, not debt. You do not owe anything in life because there is no past, there is no future, there is only this ten seconds from which you create your life.

- Place in front of you the mantra: **"All of life comes to me with ease and joy and glory."**

- Say, **"I am power, I am awareness, I am control, I am creativity, I am money,"** ten times in the morning, ten times in the evening.

- Put it somewhere, where you see it and share it with others, **"I allow the abundant universe to provide me with a multiplicity of opportunities all designed to encompass and support my growth, my awareness and my joyful expression of life."** And be it, because that is the truth of you.

And, so, enough this night. Be money in every aspect of life. We leave you in love. Good night.

ACCESS CONSCIOUSNESS®

ALL OF LIFE COMES TO ME WITH EASE AND JOY AND GLORY!

www.accessconsciousness.com

www.ingramcontent.com/pod-product-compliance
Lightning Source LLC
Chambersburg PA
CBHW081509200326
41518CB00015B/2434

* 9 7 8 1 6 3 4 9 3 0 1 9 2 *